CONFESSIONS

of an

ELEMENTARY SCHOOL PRINCIPAL

MERIL R. SMITH

Nathan Hatch, Illustrator

This book is a series of anecdotes collected
over a wonderful career in education.

PAGE PUBLISHING, INC.
Conneaut Lake, PA

First originally published by Page Publishing 2019

All anecdotes are true.
Only some of the names have been changed to protect the guilty.
Also, all proceeds from this book are donated to the Edenvale
Elementary School Adopt-A-College scholarship fund.

ISBN 978-1-64584-780-9 (pbk)
ISBN 978-1-64584-781-6 (digital)

Printed in the United States of America

I have been awed and inspired by youngsters,
especially those who attend Edenvale School,
and by the teachers who truly believe
they can and do make the difference in each youngster's life.

For over a half century, I have enjoyed
the love and support of Barbara Forkash Smith.

For being humbled and inspired by my children:
Rachel Esther Smith
Leah Amy Smith

For the love I share with
grandchildren and great-grandchildren:
Brennen Mathew Smith
Kyle Evans Smith-Doolittle
Laura Elizabeth Smith-Doolittle
Ari Evelio Feder
Brahm Juniper Feder
Michael Laney
Julien Smith Close
Danielle Allen-Coover
Elijah Coy Coover

In honor of my three mentors:
Jerry Schmidt
Delos "Ace" Bagby
Anthony P. Russo

CONTENTS

INTRODUCTION

Who? Me?

For some reason, after retiring from a wonderful career in education, I started asking questions: who am I, really? What happened? Why me? I am not sure why I started thinking about these questions… Perhaps it is because of advancing age. Perhaps it is that I am worried that I will start forgetting things. Perhaps it is wondering if the events throughout my life made any difference.

Two simple principles have guided me.

> "Treat every person with dignity and respect…no matter what!"

> "*TIKKUN OLAM*: heal, repair, and transform the world."

Everything else has been commentary.

Both of my parents were born in California, and I was born in 1943. My parents grew up during the Great Depression of the 1930s. One set of grandparents lost everything they owned, and my grandmother found work as a maid. The lack of food during the depression deeply affected my parents, millions of other people, and how their generation lived the rest of their lives. People in my parents' generation had an obsession with storing food.

Growing up, my family was dirt-poor. Frequently the shelves in the pantry were nearly empty. When the pantry was not stocked with canned goods and dry goods, it drove my mother "crazy." The effects of the depression brought my parents together. They met in high school and married very young. They did not have any money or job skills, but "they had each other."

After World War II, my father became a carpenter...a good carpenter. When the weather was good, he worked. When it rained, my father did not work. Each week he did not work, the pantry became emptier and my mother worried. In 1950, my parents bought a small piece of property surrounded by prune, apricot, and cherry orchards. Dad built a small two-bedroom, one-bath house. My beloved grandmother lived in a room behind the garage.

To help make sure the family had food, we had a large vegetable garden and raised chickens and rabbits. In addition, my parents always hid a large case of elbow macaroni and a large bag of rice... just in case. "Just in case" happened quite often. Dad bought sacks of chicken feed and rabbit pellets from the feed store. My mother took the feed sacks and made shirts for me to wear to school. I hated wearing those feed sack shirts.

The school bus chugged through the orchards every day, stopped at each house, and took us to school. The same bus brought us home each afternoon. I liked the long ride through the orchards. I learned a lot riding the bus. The parents of a few of the kids owned orchards. Many of my friends were kids of farm workers. Other friends were kids whose families had been released from the concentration camps. Many of the Japanese American kids were living in war surplus metal Quonset huts. I did not know why, but I just felt something was wrong with the idea that some of my friends were living in metal huts while most us lived in some kind of a house. Years later, when I was one of three whites attending an all-black college in Virginia, I began to understand about hatred and discrimination.

At school, I was one of the dumb kids. I did not learn to read until sixth grade. Jerry Schmidt, my sixth-grade teacher, pulled me aside at the beginning of the year and said to me, "Meril, you are going to learn to read this year, or we are both going to die trying." I believed him. I was not ready to die. I did learn to read.

Jerry Schmidt really believed in me, and I never forgot it. His belief in me changed the course of my life. It was because of Jerry that I did not drop out of high school. I somehow got into college. I struggled in college. I failed. I started over. It wasn't until my fourth year in college that I realized that I wanted to be like Jerry Schmidt; I wanted to become a teacher. That realization was the beginning of me having a focus and doing well in college.

In closing, growing up poor helped me see other people in a kinder and more accepting way than I might have otherwise. No matter our race or religious beliefs, many of us grew up wearing the same shoes...shoes with holes in them.

Part 1

Learning to Be a
Teacher
(1964–1966)

It's OK, Mr. Wallace

In 1964, I was a student teacher. Being a student teacher was a time to practice in the classroom what had been learned in college and, at the same time, be under the guidance of a master teacher. Ron Wallace was truly a master teacher.

Ron had a wonderful relationship with students. There was no doubt that he was the *teacher* and was in complete control of his classroom. Ron was a master teacher, both content and instructional strategies. Students really liked Ron and they always respected him. When he spoke, students listened...and when he taught, students learned.

For most of the semester, I saw Ron teach. Every day was filled with new and valuable experiences. The most important thing I began to learn was how to control a classroom of students, not trying to be their "friend," or having to be a heavy-handed *disciplinarian* but by becoming a skilled user of classroom management techniques.

As part of student teaching, I just watched the class and took notes for two weeks. Then I started by teaching a lesson or two each day. Soon Ron had me assume responsibility for one subject and teach that subject every day. A couple of weeks later, Ron gave me responsibility for several subjects. Finally, it was time to go solo and take over the class for two whole weeks. The first few days of my solo teaching, Ron was in the back of the room working at his desk. Then he left, and I was on my own for the next week. Some of my lessons went well and others not so well. The content was easy, but controlling the kids was harder. I really tried to put into practice what I had observed Ron doing every day and found out that his classroom management techniques really worked. Student teaching for Ron Wallace was a gift that lasted through a career of forty years.

However, this story is not about student teaching. This story is about an incident that happened one afternoon when students returned from physical education.

Remember, I was a student teacher in the 1960s, and expectations for teachers and students were quite different than they are today. Men on the staff wore slacks, a shirt and tie, and a sports coat. Women teachers had to wear dresses, nylons, and high-heeled shoes. Wearing slacks or pants was certainly not permitted. The dress code was a real challenge for women teachers who taught kindergarten and first grade. During the day, teachers often bent over to help a student or sat next to a student in a tiny, nine-inch high, student chair. Besides being a teacher, teachers also had to be contortionists. Dress codes were not limited to teachers; they also applied to students, especially girls. Girls had to wear dresses and behave in "a ladylike manner."

This day was quite warm for October. The students had been outside for physical education. It was obvious they had a good time and many were slightly sweaty.

Joanne was a lively fifth grader. She was always full of energy. On this particular day, Joanne came in from PE a bit sweaty and plopped down at her desk. She put her feet up on a nearby chair in a not very ladylike position. Obviously, in the 1960s, wearing a dress and sitting with your legs spread apart was not acceptable.

Ron Wallace looked at Joanne, saw how she was sitting, and walked over to her desk. I remember him softly saying, "Joanne, sit up the right way in your chair. Sit ladylike." Joanne looked at Mr. Wallace and, with a big smile, lifted up her dress, saying, "It's OK, Mr. Wallace. I have pants on underneath my dress."

That was the day I learned to be slow to judge as well as see the humor in what students say and do. Ron Wallace gave me the beginnings of becoming a good educator.

Life Lesson: Not everyone sees things the same as I do. I try looking at what is going on around me with different lenses. Eyeglasses with different lenses often help me see better.

Never Be Alone!

The day I finished student teaching at Sartorette Elementary School, I was offered a job at the same school. A fourth-grade teacher would be on sick leave until the end of the school year. What an opportunity! Thrilled was an understatement!

At twenty-one years old, I not only had my own class but also just few doors away was Ron Wallace for whom I had worked as a student teacher. In addition, there were two additional male teachers from whom I could learn—Bud Owens and Bob Schultz.

Having my own class of students was an amazing experience. The classroom management skills I learned from Ron Wallace really paid off. Since I did not know the curriculum for fourth grade, I studied and prepared six lessons each evening. I kept ahead of the students by one day. At lunchtime, the four male teachers would often sit together and share what was happening. We often laughed. Bob Schultz teased me about being a beginning teacher. Bob teased me about being just twenty-one. His teasing was always good-natured. It made me feel part of the group. Teaching was exciting!

Bob Schultz had a sixth grade student that had physically matured very, very early. Alison was a delightful girl who looked more like a college student than a sixth grader. Apparently, Bob decided that it was time for me to learn an important lesson about being a teacher.

It was a Wednesday. The school day had just ended, and the last of my students was out the door. A few minutes later, I was surprised when there was a knock at the door. When I opened the door, there stood Alison in a very tight sweater!

A bit confused, I asked Alison, "How can I help you?"

Alison replied, "I am here to help you out. Mr. Schultz said you had a lot of work to do." I did have a lot of papers to grade and also needed time to prepare for tomorrow's lessons.

Fortunately, a bell went off and red lights began flashing in my mind. How would it look if a twenty-one-year-old teacher was alone in a classroom with a girl who looked eighteen? I had to think on my feet. While still standing at the door, I replied, "Thank you, Alison, for offering to help me out. However, I just finished most of the things I need to do. Hope you have a great afternoon. Thanks again." Alison left, and I let out a big sigh of relief. Thanks to Bob Schultz, I learned the following lesson firsthand.

Life Lesson: If students stay after school, always keep the door open. Most importantly, never be in a classroom alone with a girl... It could end a career!

Barf Bucket, Anyone?

As a result of the World War II and the Korean War GI Bills, huge numbers of men went to college, good jobs were available, and the size of the American middle class exploded. In 1957, the Soviet Union launched Sputnik, the first human-made satellite to orbit the earth. Sputnik shocked the United States, and the resulting space race caught schools and educators unprepared. Overnight math and science replaced language arts as the priority. It was also a time when being a teacher was really exciting.

The Santa Clara Valley was a hub for the aerospace industry. Ford-Philco, IBM, Lockheed, and Fairchild led a booming economy. The space race resulted in engineers flocking to San Jose to thousands of jobs in what would soon be called Silicon Valley. In the Santa Clara Valley, the space race was very serious business and soon replaced an agricultural economy based upon prunes, cherries, apricots, and pears that I grew up with. Then President John F. Kennedy announced in 1962 that the United States would put a man on the moon. Many people thought getting a rocket to the moon was improbable and landing a man on the moon was impossible!

It was during the height of the space race when I became a teacher. Although the Vietnam War was raging in the 1960's, it was beyond any imagining that I would be drafted or a few years later become a spacecraft controller.

In 1969, I was assigned to Site Alpha in Diyarbakir, Turkey. By some good fortune, I was able play a small role in the Apollo 11 mission when Neil Armstrong landed on the moon.

From the Apollo 11 experience, I realized that we "turn many corners" during our lives. We are often surprised at what we find "around the corner." We never really know what awaits us until we make the turn. Many corners have appeared in my life, none better than the corner I turned that led me to teaching.

Teaching fourth grade at Sartorette Elementary School in 1965 was my first teaching assignment. Sartorette was located in a middle-class neighborhood in San Jose, California. Although the school was built in response to an exploding population, fueled by the space race, Sartorette School was pure 1950s. The elementary school curriculum was teacher-directed and centered on passive learning of language arts and arithmetic skills.

Most classrooms were designed for students to sit in rows and work quietly at their desks. On one side of the room, there were large windows that opened for ventilation…no such thing as air conditioning. Large chalkboards were clear across the front of the room. Beautiful wooden cabinets and a sink were across the back of the room. The remaining wall had small windows at the top (to create cross ventilation) and a very large bulletin board on which teachers displayed student work. In the 1950s and 1960s, students sat at miniature desks. The floors were tiles, polished several times a year to a high sheen.

Classrooms were also designed for the technology in use at the time. The 1950s classroom technology consisted of an overhead projector and a 16 mm movie projector. Each classroom had two—*just two*—electrical plugs. One electrical plug was in the front of the classroom directly below the center of the chalkboard...for the overhead projector. The other one was in the back of the room for the 16 mm movie projector. That electrical plug was *directly above the water faucet*. To this day, I still wonder why no one was ever electrocuted.

A school curriculum was centered on language arts and arithmetic. In 1958, the sudden shift to math and science, in our rush to win the space race, did not match very well with the design of most school classrooms. Could anything be done to modify pre-space race classrooms to help bring them in line with the new push in math and science?

As a beginning teacher, fresh from the university, it was not hard to come up with several ways to change a classroom.

- In addition to fiction library books, add lots of books about scientists, inventions, and the amazing discoveries being made.
- In math, focus on thinking skills and problem-solving that go far beyond simple computation. How math was taught was revolutionized by the School Mathematic Study Group curriculum and materials developed by the National Science Foundation.
- Introduce biology by bringing small animals into the classroom. Although not intended, two white rats and a non-poisonous snake soon become classroom pets.

- Change how desks were arranged, from straight rows to four desks being pushed together, to form a worktable. That way, students had an easier way to work in teams.
- Use experiments and projects in ways that enabled students to learn together instead of in isolation as individuals. However, working together did increase the noise level in the room.
- Since sound tends to bounce off hard surfaces, I purchased a very large, medium-brown carpet. The carpet helped absorb sound and decrease the level of noise.

Even though we found new ways of teaching math and science, the way language arts were taught remained the same. In most elementary schools, the first two hours of the morning continued to focus on language arts. However, when it came to math and science, it was a new ball game. In math and science, students were often actively involved in learning concepts. Sometimes students were required to get out of their seats, talk to each other, and work together. Fourth graders were excited about learning in new and different ways. They were intellectually challenged to use the higher-level thinking skills that were needed. Student became active rather than passive learners. Youngsters were challenged, and much of the time, learning became fun.

In the spring of 1966, some kind of "bug" hit the school, and students would suddenly "turn green." Since our room was directly across from the restrooms, the classroom door was left open just in case someone got sick. "If you suddenly feel like you are going to throw up, get to the restroom. You do not need to ask permission, just go. I understand." After throwing up, students would be sent to the nurse's office and most likely sent home.

The system worked well until one fateful day. After lunch, teams of students were working on a science project. I was walking around, checking in with each team to see how they were doing, and offering suggestions if they were stuck. As I was moving from group to group, Eric suddenly got up.

Although Eric had red hair and freckles, his face was sickly green. He took three steps toward the door...

Remember that new large medium-brown carpet? The carpet worked well because some of the noise created by active learners was now absorbed by the carpet.

Apparently as part of his lunch, Eric drank a juice drink...a bright red juice drink. After taking three steps toward the door, Eric was right in the middle of the carpet. Eric didn't make it. Bright red vomit hurled from his mouth and landed right on the center of the carpet!

That night, I came back to school with carpet cleaning supplies. The vomit was easy to clean up...but the stain would not come out. The bright red stain was permanent.

The next morning, a five-gallon barf bucket sat right on top of the bright red stain. "If you have to throw up and cannot make it to the restroom, use the barf bucket." For some reason, no one ever used the barf bucket. However, the bright red stain was still there at the end of the school year when I was drafted into the military.

Lucy and Norman

This event happened at Sartorette Elementary School in the spring of 1966. The second year of teaching fourth grade was fantastic! My first year was spent learning the content of each subject and trying to stay one day ahead of the students. By the second year, I was familiar with subject content and had developed some good instructional techniques. The class of thirty-two youngsters was a dream come true. To be sure, a few students were challenging, but I was able to get down to the business of teaching.

In the primary grades, the emphasis is teaching students the basic skills of "reading, writing, and arithmetic." By the time students are in fourth grade, most youngsters can unlock new words, write complete sentences and basic paragraphs, as well as add and subtract.

Fourth graders are delightful. In fourth grade, students put basic skills to work. Youngsters start to read to gain information and learn concepts. Writing starts to include ideas and paragraphs that are better developed. Mathematics is about starting to understand the theories behind addition, subtraction, multiplication, and division. A big focus in fourth grade mathematics is beginning to learn how to analyze and solve word problems.

Best of all, fourth graders develop a real sense of humor. Not "Ha ha!" funny humor but humor using words, double meanings, and twists. I remember one joke that could crack up the class every time someone asked me, "What is big and red and eats rocks?" I would always have a puzzled look on my face and shrug my shoulders. The entire class would respond in unison, "A big red rock eater!" There is a lot to be said for comic relief.

Norman was energetic, to say the least. He delighted in doing things that would distract neighboring students and get them off task. I frequently moved Norman to a different place in the room with different students sitting next to him; the result never changed.

Lucy was a selective mute. She was very smart and extremely self-disciplined. Lucy had the ability to talk but seldom said anything to other kids and never talked to an adult.

I had a brilliant idea! Move Norman to the front row and the far left corner. No students would sit in front of him, and Norman would be close to where I frequently stood. There would be only one person sitting next to him...on his right side. I moved Lucy next to Norman. Absolutely brilliant, it worked! Norman's antics were contained.

A few weeks later, it was time for a math test. The end-of-unit test required students to really think and use a variety of skills to solve the math problems.

For me, this was a very important test. I would be able to analyze how students answered each problem. More importantly, it would help me determine what I needed to reteach.

Recess was over. Before entering the classroom, I said to the students, "When you go into the room, go directly to your desk and sit down. There is a math test on your desk. The test is upside down. Do not touch the test or turn it over until I tell you to do so."

Everyone knew this was serious business. Youngsters walked into the classroom and sat quietly at their desks. I walked to the front of the room, near where Noman sat, and gave instructions.

"During this math unit, we have been learning different ways to solve problems. This is a very important test for you and for me. I want you to take your time and do your personal best. When I grade your test, I will see what you have learned and what I need to reteach."

"Some of you may finish sooner than others. It's not important how fast you work but how carefully you think and solve each problem. Take your time, you have lots of time. There is no need to hurry. When you are finished, turn your test upside down."

"Now take out your library book and put it on the corner of your desk. If you finish before others, read your library book. Do not disturb anyone around you. *I do not want to hear a sound* until everyone has finished the test and I have collected them."

The directions were clear and specific. The students knew I was serious. With that, I told the students to turn over their tests and begin. I walked toward the back of the room to sit at my desk and watch the class take the test. I had almost reached my desk when I heard a student in uproarious laughter.

I had just told the class that I did not want to hear a sound until the test was over. Steam came out of my ears! I whirled around to find out from where the laughter was coming. That youngster was going to get a piece of my mind!

I scanned the room. To my utter amazement, the laughter was coming from Lucy. Apparently, Norman had done something that really cracked up Lucy. Lucy was laughing so hard she couldn't help herself. My anger melted. My heart smiled. I turned back around and, without a word, walked to my desk and sat down. Hearing Lucy laugh made my day, my week, my month, and my year.

Life Lesson: Sometimes the smallest things are the most enjoyable.

Teacher Gets a Grade: D-

The second year of teaching was even better than the first. The six to eight lessons for each day were thought out and written. Worksheets and projects were dittoed and stacked in order. On the large bulletin board, student work was prominently displayed. The room was orderly and had been adapted for the space race push for more math and science. Youngsters frequently worked together in small groups and were actively involved in learning. They were learning and having fun. However, my desk was usually a mess with stacks of papers to be graded, materials for lessons, and books, lots of books.

The principal of Sartorette School was Sal Colletto. Sal was definitely in charge. He had high expectations for both teachers and students. The school was organized and well run. Sal was always supportive of his staff. In addition, Sal had a nice sense of humor and was quick to smile or laugh. As a beginning teacher, I was fortunate that someone like Sal Colletto was my first principal.

Every Friday, teachers submitted lesson plans for the following week. Sal actually read them, wrote comments, and had them in your mailbox by the time you arrived on Monday. Lesson plans were always to be in plain sight on the teacher's desk. Sal wanted each room to be a rich and inviting learning environment…with motivational sayings on the wall and lots of books in the classroom library.

He believed in having at least one piece of each student's work displayed on the bulletin board as a way of acknowledging youngsters' efforts. Sal's expectations also included that the room be organized and tidy.

Since I was a beginning teacher, Sal also did a lot of drop-in observations as well as the formal observations during the year. For formal observations, Sal would tell me what subject area he wanted to see me teach. We would set up a day and time. Before the actual observation, Sal required a written copy of the lesson plan. Then we held a meeting to discuss the concepts included in the lesson and the methods I was going to use. Sal always wanted to know how I was going to measure student learning.

He frequently visited my classroom. Often the informal drop-in observations lasted five or ten minutes. The students enjoyed it when Sal dropped in. If I wasn't actively teaching, Sal would frequently engage students to find out what they were learning.

On one Wednesday morning, I arrived at school at seven o'clock. I usually arrived early to make sure everything was ready for the day before students arrived at 8:15 a.m. I remembered that a hands-on science experiment was going to be the high point of the day and I was ready.

When I walked over to my desk, I found a strange note on top of the piles of papers. Sal had apparently come into my room late at night after I went home. Was it possible that I was being graded and this was the report card?

- Lesson Plans: A
- Organized Learning Environment: A-
- Bulletin Board: A-
- Classroom Neatness: B+
- Teacher's Desk: D-

I only saw the last grade. Sal Colletto caught me and caught me big-time. My desk *was* a mess. It looked chaotic. In my defense, I could always find everything, but the desk was something that needed improvement, a lot of improvement. There was no doubt, I had definitely earned the D-.

> *Life Lesson: For the rest of my career, I worked on how my desk looked and was organized. No matter where I worked or what I did, my desk haunted me. It never got a grade above a C. Big deal! Get over it! And I did!*

I Luff You

(Barbara Forkash Smith)

Billy was a very cute little kindergartner. He had a great smile and "Coke bottle" glasses. He also had a pronounced lisp. Billy always had something to tell me—a story, a secret, or something special. He was so enthusiastic when he talked to me!

One day, Billy came running across the kindergarten playground. He was in a hurry! I was ready for him. I had a big smile waiting for Billy. He matched me with his smile.

Billy reached up and put his arms around my waist.

The first thing I saw were his "Coke bottle" lenses. His face beamed up at me as he said, "Mith Forkathhh, I luff you!"

You Have Fat Legs!

(Barbara Forkash Smith)

In the 1960s, it was hard to be a kindergarten teacher and ladylike at the same time. Women teachers were required to wear dresses and nylons. They were also required to get down to a child's level and sit in nine-inch-high chairs.

Often the children would come to the front of the room and sit on the floor while I read a story or taught a lesson. They were taught to sit "crisscross applesauce," with their hands in their laps.

Elizabeth loved to cozy up to me and be as close as she could. Before I would realize it, she would rub her hands up and down my nylon stockings. I would remove Elizabeth's hands and have her slide back to the rest of the students. Within seconds, Elizabeth would be back sitting next to me once again, rubbing her hands up and down my nylons.

One day, I firmly told Elizabeth to stop rubbing my nylons. My comment did not seem to faze her. Elizabeth scooted up again, gazed at me, and said, "Gee, Miss Forkash, you have fat legs!"

Enough was enough. I had had it! I gazed back down at Elizabeth and said softly, "Someday you will have fat legs too."

Where Oh Where Has My Student Gone?

(Barbara Forkash Smith)

The coming of Halloween stirs up much excitement in classrooms. Just mention the word *Halloween* and a buzz goes through the room. Kindergarten is no exception.

Most years I took my kindergartners to a pumpkin patch to see how pumpkins grow as well as pick out their favorite pumpkin. Permission slips are sent home to be signed and returned. Each child brought fifty cents to pay for their pumpkin. Arrangements for a bus are made. Parent volunteers are recruited. Detailed plans are required to go on a field trip.

On the day of the field trip to the pumpkin patch, the students were very excited. Each child wore a name tag and was assigned to a volunteer—six children for each volunteer. As the teacher, I oversaw and kept track of everything!

Students lined up at the door, and I counted them—twenty-nine in all. Students got on to the bus, and I counted them—twenty-nine in all. When we arrived at the pumpkin patch and got off the bus, I counted the students—twenty-nine again. All is right with the world!

The youngsters and volunteers had so much fun. The farmers divided my class and volunteers into three groups and took us on a tour. We learned all about pumpkins—from seed to sprout to blossom to mature pumpkin. Then each group of students and their volunteer went out into the field to search for their perfect pumpkin.

Some children chose small pumpkins, others chose medium pumpkins. A few chose very large pumpkins. Each student was responsible for carrying their own pumpkin to the pay station. Partway to the pay station, a couple of children with very large pumpkins changed their mind—too heavy!

Each group, along with their volunteer, paid for the pumpkins and headed for the bus. After everyone was on the bus, I counted the students again—twenty-eight. "What? Twenty-eight!" I counted again. "Twenty-eight!"

Each volunteer checked their list of names… Gregory was missing! One of the volunteers and I got off the bus and began a search for Gregory. We searched the barn, the bathrooms, the field, and the pay station. We were told by the farmer there was a creek near the pumpkin patch. The farmer went with us, and we searched up and down the creek. No Gregory! Now we were really worried. We had to return to school without Gregory. The bus driver radioed the school district and reported Gregory missing, and the bus dispatcher called the school.

The bus arrived back at the school. All the parents were waiting on the sidewalk. Each volunteer and their group got off the bus and walked to their parents, carrying their pumpkins. Gregory's mother was also on the sidewalk, and I had to tell her that Gregory was missing. Together we went to the office and started trying to figure out where Gregory was.

I had noticed that other buses were leaving the pumpkin patch at the same time. Could Gregory be on another bus?

Meanwhile, another bus from another school arrived back at their school. After they arrived, the students went back to their classroom for a story. The teacher looked down to make sure the students were ready for the story. "Who are you? Where did you come from? What school do you go to?"

The teacher immediately called down to the office, and before you could count to ten, the principal was in the doorway. Within seconds, we received a phone call saying that Gregory had been found. The principal said that with Gregory's mother's permission, he would drive Gregory back to our school. Gregory returned, and we all breathed a big sigh of relief, especially Gregory's mother!

Part 2

U.S.A.F.

Cambrian School District

Coming Home

(1970–1973)

An Offer I Couldn't Refuse

After four years in the Air Force, I was released from active duty. Although I had learned a great deal in the military, I was ready to come home and resume a teaching career.

The original Cambrian School was built in the 1930s and was located among the orchards where two roads crossed…no stores, no gas stations, no post office or other buildings. Cambrian School was truly out in the boondocks like where I grew up.

During WWII, many GIs spent time training in California before being shipped out to the war in the Pacific. Unlike many parts of the United States, California had beautiful weather, especially the ocean. After the war, many GIs started moving their young families west to the "golden state." California was the "land of opportunity." Good jobs were also in abundance.

In the 1950s, the Santa Clara Valley was rapidly changing. Semiconductors and the aerospace replaced agriculture and became the new economic engine. Sputnik and the space race resulted in a boom economy. Instead of being known as the Valley of Heart's Delight, the valley soon became known as Silicon Valley.

Cambrian Park was in the perfect geographical location for much-needed homes. Within a few years, orchards had been torn out and replaced by large tracts of new homes. The baby boom was booming, and kids needed to be educated, which meant schools, lots of new schools. In just a few years, Cambrian grew from one to ten schools.

Delos M. "Ace" Bagby was superintendent of Cambrian School District and a fascinating person. Ace had attended San Jose State College and was an athlete...a gymnast. He earned the nickname Ace because he was known to ace every landing. (Ace was still doing one-hand pushups when he was eighty years old.) He was a people person with a great handshake, an even greater smile, and a fantastic sense of humor. Ace loved people and had the unique ability to remember names...everybody's name. He even remembered the name of each employee's children, most of whom he never met. Although Ace started his career as a teacher, he soon became the principal. He was the "godfather" of Cambrian. When Cambrian School District started to grow, no one was surprised when Ace became the district's very first superintendent.

In June 1970, I found out I would be released from military service in late August, just before the start of a new school year. Under the law, people serving in the armed forces had a right to return to the same company and the same job they had before being drafted. For me, that meant being guaranteed a teaching position. Hurray!

I called Mr. Bagby immediately. Ace not only remembered me by name but also asked about my wife…again by name. When told that I was being released by the Air Force and was ready to return to teaching, he welcomed me back. Ace said that there would be a teaching position for me in September but that at the moment he was not sure about which school or grade level. He said he would call me back within a week.

A week later, Ace Bagby called with an offer. He told me about a class of "low-functioning" students who needed a good teacher. I knew that whatever job Ace offered me would be one I could not refuse.

After graduating from college, I had taken classes in special education at Virginia State College and worked with low-functioning students in my off hours while in the Air Force. However, there was no way I was qualified to teach them. There was a long pause on my end of the phone as my mind raced about how to answer. "Honestly, I am not sure how good a teacher I will be in a class of low-functioning students. However, since you think I will do a good job, I accept."

Now there was a pause on his end of the phone. "Meril, I'm not surprised at your answer. In fact, I expected it." He continued, "I also have a teaching position in the Extended Curriculum Workshop (ECW). ECW is a program for the thirty brightest fifth and sixth youngsters in the school district. You will be working with an incredible teammate, Cathy Ward. I think you are a perfect match for the program, for Cathy Ward, and for these students."

Accepting this offer was one of the best decisions I ever made.

Life Lesson: When I worked with low-functioning youngsters, I was frequently referred to as The Retarded Teacher. In the two years I spent teaching gifted children, I was never once called The Gifted Teacher. In retrospect, I guess they were right.

Undercover Reader

Soon after Ace Bagby assigned me to the Extended Curriculum Workshop (ECW), fifteen new fifth graders were also assigned to the program. Since ECW was made up of both fifth and sixth graders, the numbers of students were about the same for each grade. The IQ of the youngsters in ECW ranged from 132 to 187!

Cathy Ward, my new teammate, spent hours tutoring me about the hands-on curriculum and how the class worked. Perhaps the most important lesson was how we were expected to provide a learning environment in which these kids would thrive academically, socially, and emotionally.

Since most of the students were bussed from other schools, Cathy and I met the bus on the first day of school to be sure each youngster felt welcome. The new students looked anxious, and the returning students (now sixth graders) were great about welcoming and reassuring the new students. The sixth graders took the new fifth graders under their wings and were much more effective in helping the new students get acclimated than either Cathy or me.

It did not take long for the students attending the ECW to realize they had many of the same interests and could really discuss ideas with each other. Friendships developed quickly. It may be a strange thing to say, but in the ECW, youngsters did not have to hide their brightness.

Shortly after the start of school, Cathy and I held Back-to-School Night. We eagerly greeted parents, who were just as eager to meet us. They wanted to find out how we taught and the kind of curriculum their child would experience. One big concern centered on making friends. Parents hoped that strong friendships would develop between these very bright youngsters who often had had few friends.

A number of parents echoed the same theme. In past years, their child found it difficult to be accepted by classmates. Their interests and intellectual abilities were at a very different level than grade-level peers. Some of the kids had tried to dumb down and hide their abilities in order to be better accepted by other children.

Nothing drove this point home more than what Angela's mother, Mrs. Petty, shared a few weeks later at Angela's parent conference. Mrs. Petty shared she had been very worried about her daughter changing schools. Could Angela adjust to a different kind of program, new teachers, a new school, and new students, none of whom she knew? Although previous teachers really liked her and Angela did very well academically, she was basically a social outcast; the kids just didn't get Angela. Angela loved to read and devoured books. The books Angela read were usually several years above her grade level. As a result, some of the kids had really teased "the brain." Suddenly, Angela stopped reading books.

Not reading really concerned Mrs. Petty until she walked into Angela's bedroom one evening. Angela was completely under the covers, head too! Mrs. Petty could see the light from a flashlight. When Mrs. Petty called out to Angela, Angela emerged from under the covers with the flashlight and a book.

Then Mrs. Petty smiled and shared that Angela no longer felt the need to read under the covers. Angela had made several new friends and was having a good time sharing their mutual interests in books. Mrs. Petty said that ECW was working out well for Angela, better than she expected.

At the time, I found it hard to understand the great lengths this youngster had gone to hide both her love of books and her intelligence. Being gifted is thought to be a wonderful thing. I soon learned that being gifted, being different, also has downsides. Angela helped me to begin to understand about the importance of teaching the "whole child..." of being aware and trying to meet the social and emotional needs as well as academic needs.

Life Lesson: Learn to listen, really listen.

Wheels Instead of Hands

Every day working with the youngsters attending the Extended Curriculum Workshop was a challenge and a privilege. The challenge was making sure lessons were challenging their intellectual abilities and developing their ability to think in new and different ways. The privilege was me being one of their teachers.

When the students arrived each morning, there were routine tasks that needed to be done such as attendance, lunch count, etc. In many classrooms, this is sort of a "dead time" for students. Not in the Extended Curriculum Workshop! Each morning, students came into the classroom with a creative writing topic on the chalkboard. They had ten minutes to write a paragraph in their journal. On Fridays, youngsters could choose to share their favorite paragraph with the class.

Challenge to the reader: Write a paragraph on this topic, "What would it be like if you had wheels instead of hands?"

Life Lesson: Sometimes ideas that appear simple are actually not!

But the Planetarium Doesn't Work!

The students in the Extended Curriculum Workshop were doing a unit on astronomy with a touch of mythology. One day, the students entered the classroom to find a big wooden box...three feet square and five feet high. What was it doing in our classroom? How did a three-foot square box fit through the door? It was a mystery!

The students had recently gone on a field trip to the planetarium at the Egyptian Rosicrucian Museum. After much discussion, the class decided to use the box to build their own planetarium.

How do you build a planetarium? This was an idea that required a lot of research and planning. Part of the class focused on the mechanics of projecting stars onto a ceiling. Another group focused on physically changing the box into a planetarium.

When each group had finished planning, it was time to get to work. Since only one hour a day was allotted to the planetarium, preplanning was essential. A three-foot-high door was cut out of one side of the box. It was hinged and made light tight. Paint cloths surrounded the box. Paint trays and rollers together with flat black paint appeared. It took three days to paint the inside and outside of the soon-to-be planetarium.

Meanwhile, the group in charge of creating the projection system was busily at work. They came up with a large plastic mixing bowl that would serve as the base for projecting stars onto the ceiling. To support the projection bowl, the base would have a wooden spool, just the right size for the upside-down bowl. While some members of the group focused on wiring a light source and a way to attach the bowl onto the spool, the rest of the group worked with star charts. They overlaid star charts onto the bowl and carefully used pushpins to go through the charts and through the bowl. Very clever…they wanted to see actual constellations projected onto the ceiling.

The teams worked hard over several weeks to complete the planetarium. Everyone was very proud of their accomplishments. As soon as the system was tested, small groups of children from other classes would be invited to a planetarium show.

The day of the test was exciting. The script was well rehearsed. Carpet tiles were used as seats. The "projection device" was put in place, and several of the students went inside for the first test show.

The group emerged with faces that were crestfallen. "But the planetarium doesn't work…" Another group went inside and soon emerged. "The planetarium doesn't work." After weeks of work, one can imagine the sadness that overwhelmed these fifth and sixth graders.

It was time to talk about what was happening. Exactly what was not working? "The stars didn't come out," was their response. "There were just faint blobs of light." A lot of discussion followed. We got out a flashlight and turned off the lights. One of the students stood next to the chalkboard and shined the flashlight on it. The light was bright, just as it should be...no help. As he walked away from the chalkboard, one of the students noticed that the area of light got bigger, but the brightness of the light became less and less.

Was something like this happening inside the planetarium? It was time to do some more research. (Remember, in 1973, there were no iPhones, no laptops, no personal computers...just books, lots of books.) The students had learned to work together to solve problems. Immediately, they formed small groups of three or four, put their minds together, and started looking in all kinds of books. It didn't take long before a student shouted out, "We found it. We know what is wrong." Everyone gathered around, and an entry from the encyclopedia was read: "The Properties of Light."

Time was up. It was the end of the school day and time to get on the bus and go home. I had never seen these students so dejected. One can only imagine the discussion around the dinner table that night.

The next day was a solemn day. Instead of standing in front of the class, I took a chair and sat among the students. Some of the students shared their conversations around the dinner table. They explained what they had learned from their parents about how light worked. Without optical lenses to focus each beam of "starlight," the planetarium simply could not work.

A couple of students shared they had gone outside and looked at the stars shining down. How beautiful the stars were shining down from the night sky...shining down. Slowly a solution developed.

For the next few days, students once again used the star charts. The kids put two large tables together to make a large enough work area.

They needed their abilities to use math, rulers, and dividers. Students needed new skills to calculate ratios and distances. Before each decision, they checked and rechecked calculations. These fifth and sixth graders worked slowly and deliberately. One team realized they needed to control the amount of light. Someone brought a rheostat from home and wired it into the control system. Finally, the changes were finished and installed.

Small groups of students took turns going into the planetarium to run tests. When they were finished, students gathered together and announced to me, "It works! The planetarium really works!" A collective cheer echoed through the classroom. "It works!"

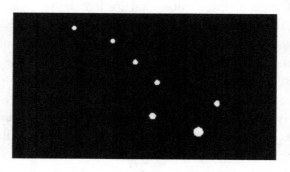

My question to the reader is: how did these fifth- and sixth-grade students solve the problem? Give it some thought...

Life Lesson: Building a planetarium was about the journey and the learning that took place. It was about working together and problem-solving. Those things were what was important...not a perfect planetarium.

Rock-a-Bye Baby

Learning to work together to solve problems and to develop social skills was a major part of the Extended Curriculum Workshop program. Helping students to share what they learned with others was one technique we used. Each month the class put on a luncheon and invited special guests—a few parents, the principal, or someone they wanted to honor.

A different planning committee of three or four students volunteered each month. The planning committee had to come up with a theme, a menu, invitations, and decorations. As planning progressed, many other students helped complete tasks. The biggest challenge in 1971 was putting on a luncheon for forty people on a budget of five dollars. (Remember, bread cost only 25 cents a loaf.)

In the spring of 1972, the students found out that Barbara and I were expecting a baby. Elizabeth (see the story, "You Have Fat Legs") was especially excited. "We have to have a shower for Mrs. Smith!" Elizabeth's committee attacked the idea with zeal. After a few days, the committee approached me. "We cannot put on a shower with a budget of $5. We need $10." After much convincing, I finally gave in. "OK, $10 cash, but that is all!"

A few days later, the committee met with me again. "We know you said that $10 for the luncheon was the limit. We also want to get some shower gifts for Mrs. Smith. Can we collect money from each other and our parents to buy some gifts?" I thought and answered, "No. $10 cash and that's it."

The next day, the committee met with me again. "How about if we collect books of S&H Green Stamps and Blue Chip Stamps?" In the 1960s and 1970s, many stores would give out stamps as premiums when you paid for your purchase. The stamps were put into little books, and the books were saved. When enough books were saved, people went to the premium store and redeemed books for all kinds of merchandise. The baby shower committee was persistent, creative, and persuasive. As a result, I agreed that since the stamp books were not cash, they could be used. I had absolutely no idea how many books of stamps would be collected…over a hundred books.

The day of the baby shower arrived. As the kids came into the room, many of them were carrying beautifully wrapped gifts—some small boxes and two very large boxes. They were so excited and all dressed up in party clothes. After morning recess, they transforming the classroom into a party room.

Crêpe paper and balloons decorated the walls. Desks were pushed together to form tables for four. Decorated placemats made out of school construction paper and centerpieces magically appeared from hiding places.

On each placemat was a dittoed party booklet created by the planning committee. The cover was a student-drawn tree holding a baby in a cradle. The title was "Rock-a-Bye Baby" surrounded by music notes.

The first pages were acknowledgments: a luncheon by Elizabeth Williams, Karen Swensen, and Dee Dee Brown. Waitresses are Laurel LeBaron and Patty Mullins. Waiters are Bill Bretschneider and Steve Silver.

The rest of the pages of the program were the menu, recipes, and student-drawn illustrations.

- Frankfurters
- Macaroni Salad
- Sourdough Bread
- Anniversary Punch
- Apple Cake

(Yes, with a lot of creativity and initiative, the committee stayed within their $10 cash budget.)

After a delicious luncheon, it was time for Barbara to open baby presents. Barbara opened the small presents first: baby lotion, baby soap, hairbrush, hooded towels, and diapers. Last to be opened was the two large presents: a baby stroller and a high chair! All the presents had been purchased using S&H and Blue Chip Stamp books!

The memory that stands out most was the four servers—the girls dressed like they were little babies going to a party and the two sixth-grade boys dressed up wearing diapers!

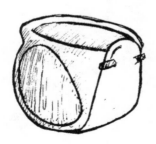

Life Lesson: Forty-six years later, we are still amazed at what eleven- and twelve-year-olds were able to accomplish. These students had learned to think out of the box. They had learned to work together and they had learned how to solve problems.

This group of youngsters was able to accomplish amazing things, even with the limitations imposed on them. They were able to go above and beyond expectations because they were passionate about what they were doing.

The Extended Curriculum Workshop's fifth and sixth graders created special memories for Barbara and me that have lasted a lifetime.

Part 3

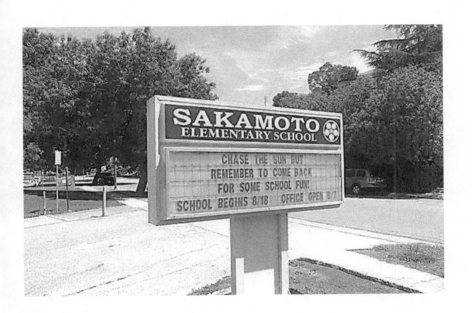

A Principalship
(1974–1979)

Sakamoto School

Two wonderful things happened to me in 1974. On Father's Day, Barbara presented me with a second beautiful daughter we named Leah. When the nurse handed me this little bundle, I fell in love all over again. In that moment, a special lifelong bond was created.

The second wonderful thing that happened was that I became a principal at thirty-one years old. Thirty-one was an amazing young age to become a principal. After learning from a number of excellent principals, it was my turn. Wow!

Oak Grove School District had been growing leaps and bounds. In twenty-five years, the district had expanded from one school, with five teachers and 150 students, to a district with many schools and over 11,000 students. With the coming of IBM to San Jose, school buildings could not be built fast enough. Sometimes two schools shared a single building. Double session was the norm until new schools were finished and students could move into the building (often new schools were actually opened in the middle of the year).

Dr. Leonard Herman had started as a principal after WWII and, when the district started to grow, became the superintendent. He was a quiet man with a vision of creating an educational system that met the needs of a rapidly changing world.

Dr. Herman worked hard to hire good people, teachers and administrators. New programs to meet the "new age" were acquired and implemented. With such rapid opening of new schools, principals needed a specific set of skills to staff a new school, get a building furnished and functional, work out the bugs, and create a sense of community around a new school.

When I was hired, the building frenzy was slowing down. Instead of principals who knew how to manage getting a new school building operational, there was now a need for principals with strong curriculum and instruction backgrounds. One of the first principals in Oak Grove School District with those skills was me. I was in the right place at the right time…and turned the corner for a lifetime of new experiences.

Life Lesson: Being a principal is a tough job. Thank goodness I had Tony Russo, a good mentor and coach!

Taking On a Veteran

Although Sakamoto Elementary was a nearly new school, I was the third principal in five years. The first year as the new principal, my focus was on getting to know students, establishing a relationship with the staff, and being visible in the community. There were also two different language arts programs and new materials to learn.

The staff consisted mostly of veteran teachers. I cannot remember if there were any first- or second-year teachers on the staff. Having experienced teachers was certainly an advantage. As a first-year principal, there was a lot I didn't know!

Spending time in classrooms was very important. Most days, I would informally drop into a couple of classrooms and just watch for a few minutes. Usually, I wrote a short note after my visit, focusing on something positive I observed.

By the second year, I had learned the ropes. A good relationship was being established with both the staff and students. I had a good knowledge of the curricular and instructional programs in the school. Although most of the staff were accomplished teachers, I began to have concerns about two teachers.

Emily had taught for about twenty years. She had a history of changing schools every few years. Emily started teaching long before Sputnik and the space race. She was strictly old school. Emily's approach to teaching was authoritarian, and she was a strict disciplinarian. At times she appeared vindictive and other times just plain mean. Students were often put down or ridiculed if they made mistakes. Woe be it to any third grader who crossed Emily.

During my third year, Emily and I were having serious discussions about the way she taught. She told we what she believed and why. I certainly had no reason to question her knowledge of curriculum or what students need to learn. I did have big concerns about the way Emily was treating students. When she took students to task for making a mistake, I saw them slump or hang their heads. In my opinion, her discipline and treatment of youngsters were harmful and emotionally damaging.

As a person, I have never liked confrontation. How I approach concerns has always been important to me. Asking questions and trying to understand another point of view has always seemed a better way to deal with problems. However, in our discussions, Emily found ways to absolutely dismiss any of my concerns. After all, she had taught a long time and knew what she was doing. Most teachers have the ability to step back and look at things from more than one point of view. That is normal. What I heard from Emily was not normal!

What was really happening? What was really going in Emily's classroom? I started dropping into her class more often and doing formal observations on a more scheduled basis. A total of four formal observations were held during that year.

How did a formal evaluation work? After a date and time was established for a formal observation, a pre-observation conference was required. The concepts and approaches to be used as a part of the lesson were discussed. A copy of the written lesson plan was given to the principal. The observation took place, and using the lesson plan as a guide, the principal took notes. After the observation, a post-conference was held. Both the teacher and the principal discussed what happened during the lesson in detail, what went well and what might be done differently. After the post-conference, a conference summary was then written, given to the teacher, and signed by both. The teacher also had the right to add additional comments to the summary. The finalized conference summary was used in part to prepare the teacher's yearly evaluation.

Again, there was never a concern about the content or the concepts contained in Emily's lessons. The concerns centered on how she managed the class, how she interacted, and how she treated individuals. Her negativity toward students really bothered me. During one of the formal observations, I kept score of the number of comments

Emily made. In a forty-five-minute lesson, the result was a staggering fifty-one negative comments and seven positive comments.

We had a formal post-observation conference. When the tally of negative versus positive comments was shared, Emily totally denied them. How Emily treated students was unacceptable and damaging. My tact went out the window. I directed Emily to start charting every time she made a negative comment to a student. She protested and I insisted. "If you cannot keep track using a pencil and paper, keep track by making tally marks on your hand!" Emily never did track her negative comments, but I did continue to keep tallies during every classroom visit.

Principal training paid off. I had been taught to write conference summaries. I had learned to keep and date written notes during drop-in visits as well as formal observation. I knew how to be able to pull notes and summaries forward so they would be used as part of the end-of-the-year evaluation.

I had given Emily dated summaries of both informal and formal observation as they occurred throughout the year. When it came time to write Emily's formal evaluation, I specifically referenced observation summaries, drop-in notes, and discussions. I was very careful in the words I used in her evaluation. Although the end-of-the-year evaluation contained positive comments, it also included specific documentation about how she treated students. In the end, Emily was formally put on remediation for the next school year. Emily was furious!

Under the California Education Code, a teacher has ten days to add comments to an evaluation before it is finalized, submitted to the district office, and placed in the teacher's permanent personnel file.

Emily angrily informed me that she would be writing a rebuttal that I had to attach to her evaluation. A few days later, Emily gave me her attachment. Her three page diatribe was brutal, both personally and professionally. The personal attack really hurt!

The next day, I kept an appointment with Norm Menzie, Assistant Superintendent of Human Resources. When I entered Norm's office, I was totally dejected. I felt as if I had been in a boxing match with Emily and lost.

After sharing the process I had used to develop the final evaluation, Norm asked to read it. I handed the evaluation to him, and he leaned back in his chair. Norm looked grim and did not say a word. He read and read. I felt even worse as I watched him read what I wrote and what Emily wrote in response.

It felt like an hour to me, but I am sure it was only a few minutes. Norm sat bolt upright and put the evaluation on the desk in front of him. I was shaking as he looked at me. Norm said, "As bad as this sounds, Emily has done you the biggest possible favor. Your evaluation is clear and complete. You have observed Emily teach, both informally and formally. You have kept and dated notes and conference summaries. You have documented your observations and spelled out your concerns about how she treats students." A feeling of relief flooded over me.

Norm finally smiled. "As a beginning principal, you did a fine job in documenting and evaluating Emily. In her response, Emily threw the "kitchen sink" at you. Emily attacked you both professionally and personally, and you took her attack totally personally. Emily's attack is not about you. What Emily wrote reflects much more on her than it does on you." Norm's final comment was, "If Emily ends up before a hearing officer in a termination case, her own diatribe will seal her fate." Emily did not return the following year.

> *Life Lesson: "TIKKUN: heal, repair, and transform the world," if only one person at a time.*

Helicopter Gunships!

The Vietnam War was ending. Many Vietnamese were fleeing as fast as they could and any way they could get out. I remember the iconic picture of the last helicopter lifting off the United States embassy. Vietnamese, who had worked at the embassy, were hanging on to the skids of the helicopter in a desperate effort to escape.

Sakamoto Elementary School was one of the first schools in San Jose to receive the children of Vietnamese refugees. The children were suddenly in a strange country. They spoke no English. After years of experiencing war, most of the children were confused and very afraid. Fortunately, Tom, one of the teachers at Sakamoto, had served as a translator in the army and spoke fluent Vietnamese. Tom was a lifesaver!

Soon after the Vietnamese children started attending Sakamoto School, a fruit fly invasion rampaged throughout the county. Fruit flies were a real danger to California agriculture. County officials were hard-pressed about what to do. Helicopters were modified with spray rigs. For several weeks, helicopters flew in designated patterns back and forth, spraying insecticides. Sakamoto School was right at the end of one of the patterns where helicopters turned around for the next spray run.

When the Vietnamese children heard a helicopter, they immediately dove under a desk. If they heard a helicopter at home, they immediately dove under a bed. Initially, teachers had no idea what was happening. Thank goodness for Tom. Tom explained, "To Vietnamese children, the sound is the same as the helicopter gunships that would fly low over villages and machine-gun people. Hiding was the way these young children have been taught to survive."

Life Lesson: These small refugees taught me to try and look things through the eyes and experience of others, not just my own.

Miss Wiggins

The Carol Burnett Show was on television from 1967 to 1978. Many of her sketches are legendary and are just as funny today as the day they were aired. A favorite thing was watching sketches in which Tim Conway deviated from a script and what had been rehearsed. Tim Conway would change something, just a little bit. He had a way of getting to Harvey Korman, and no matter how hard Harvey struggled to keep a straight face, he would eventually crack up. Although the skits were funny, watching Harvey Korman trying not to crack up was even funnier.

One sketch series involved Tim Conway playing Mr. Tudball, a hapless boss, and Carol Burnett playing his secretary, Miss Wiggins. Miss Wiggins drove Mr. Tudball crazy doing her nails and then not being able to answer the phone because her nails were still wet. She wore a skirt so tight that her butt stood out and controlled the way she walked. Miss Wiggins was always doing her nails and going to lunch early. She was certainly not someone you would want greeting people as they walked in the door. As someone wrote, "Miss Wiggins was a bimbo that the IQ fairy never visited."

To many people, Miss Wiggins was uproariously funny. Not me. When I first became a principal, Miss Wiggins was my secretary. Like Mr. Tudbill's office, my office also had a large window that faced Miss Wiggins's desk. She also drove me crazy. In addition to taking her time answering the phone, she would often not look up from her desk when parents entered the office and would make them wait to be acknowledged. Perhaps these comments are sufficient to begin to "paint the picture."

After two years, one of us was going to leave. I said to the assistant superintendent of personnel, "It does not matter who leaves, but one of us is going to leave."

Fortunately, Miss Wiggins was reassigned, and I spent three more years at Sakamoto School.

Life Lesson: Sometimes enough is too much!

Fuck

As I mentioned earlier, Sakmoto Elementary School was one of the first schools in San Jose, California, to receive refugee children. These young refugees were suddenly in a strange country with strange customs. They spoke no English and had yet to make friends.

Bill Parker was a special education teacher. He was really tall, about six feet and eight inches, and was known by all as simply Parker. Parker stood yard duty during primary recess. Seeing little first and second graders stand next to Parker was hilarious.

Steven was a very bright second grader. He was so bright that other second graders had a hard time relating to him. Parker became Steven's friend. Steven followed Parker around the playground, and they would have wonderful conversations…at least they were wonderful for Steven.

One day, when Parker was on yard duty, he saw Steven running toward him with a little boy in tow. The little boy was one of the new Vietnamese students.

"Parker! Parker!" Steven shouted as he ran up. "Parker, I want you to meet my new friend. This is my friend, Fuck." Without flinching, Parker looked down at the little boy, shook his hand, and said, "I am glad to meet you Fuck." It was then that Parker grinned. The little boy was wearing a name tag, and Steven had used phonics to sound out his name perfectly...*Phuc.*

Life Lesson: Phonics work!

Cookbook, Anyone?

Each year the sixth graders spent a week at science camp. They observed nature up close and learned about many different kinds of plants and animals as well as the environment. Science camp was a wonderful experience for youngsters, and they came back with a greater understanding and appreciation of the natural world.

Although science camp was not expensive, there were families who simply could not afford the cost. Sometimes money would be raised through a fundraiser. Somehow we always managed to have just enough money so that every child could attend science camp.

One year, someone came up with the idea of publishing a cookbook. Parents and staff submitted their favorite recipes. For fun, we also included recipes from students. The student recipes were interspersed among the recipes submitted by adults.

My favorite recipe was submitted by a second grader.

Cooked Carrots

1. Put a bunch of carrots in a pot.
2. Put some water in the pot.
3. Put the pot on the stove.
4. *Boil the carrots for 45 minutes.*

Life Lesson: There is not a life lesson for this anecdote...just a big smile.

Abalone or the Hospital?

Let no one think otherwise, being an administrator at the district office or a principal at a school is demanding work. Every few days, there is a new challenge or a new problem with which to deal. Frequently, there are night meetings. Workdays are often twelve hours long.

In Oak Grove School District, just before the end of the school year, the administrators and spouses got together for a party. The party was held at a different house each year. The highlight of the party was a delicious dinner of fresh caught abalone. I love abalone.

One year, the party was held at a home that was similar in design to my home. The home had a step-down family room that led to a large patio. We arrived when it was still bright outside. My pupils had not yet dilated when I stepped down into the family room.

Our family room had one step. This family room had two steps. My second step was into thin air rather than the floor. My ankle twisted as I landed in a heap on the floor.

Friends immediately helped me to a chair. The pain was unbelievable. Fortunately, two nurses were at the party. Within a couple of minutes, my ankle had swollen to the size of a softball. Their recommendation was to go immediately to the emergency room and get the ankle treated.

Politely refusing, I said I would go to the emergency *after the abalone* was served. That is how much I love abalone! Despite postponing their strong recommendation, the nurses did take very good care of me. They administered anesthetics to temporally relieve the pain...several shot of good whiskey.

Life Lesson: Some people will endure a lot for abalone.

Part 4

The Very Best Years
(1987–1996)

What Should Be Done?
What Could Be Done?

By the late 1970s, Edenvale Elementary School was in bad shape. The neighborhood changed. It was no longer a "working class" neighborhood but one in which families had to struggle just to put food on the table. Poverty abounded, and drugs, gangs, and crime were everywhere. In the City of San Jose, Edenvale was labeled as "a very high-risk area."

The changes taking place in the neighborhood and the everyday effect of poverty had a huge impact on the staff. Soon the staff started to believe that kids in the Edenvale neighborhood could not really amount to anything and they were just glorified babysitters. Many staff members came to work in jeans or bib overalls. Discarded bench seats from automobiles were in many classrooms as a place for kids to look at library books. Staff members no longer believed they could really make any difference. Staff morale hit an all-time low.

As a result of the work done at Sakamoto Elementary School, I had been promoted to the Director of Instruction for all of Oak Grove School District. Some of the practices at Edenvale raised major concerns at the district level. Could anything be done to turn the school around? Late one afternoon, the superintendent, assistant superintendent, and I met with the principal. According to the principal, everything in the school was "just fine." After two and a half hours, the three of us walked out into the night in total frustration. Edenvale School had to be turned around. Whatever was done had to be big, dramatic, and effective.

If the situation had not been so dire, the superintendent would have laughed at my suggestion. "The best thing we could do at

73

Edenvale would be to evacuate the students, lock the staff inside, and blow up the building." My comment was not received well but did get us to really think about what needed to happen.

A year later, I left Oak Grove and was hired in another district as the assistant superintendent; however, that's another story.

After leaving Oak Grove School District, I lost track of what was happening at Edenvale School. A couple of years later, I found out that a new principal, Henry Castanada, had been assigned to the school. I learned the superintendent had given Henry a very specific assignment… "Clean the house!" Cleaning up the physical plant was one thing. Cleaning out the "reluctant dragons" on the staff, those who were unwilling to make changes, was quite another.

In his five years at Edenvale School, Henry did an amazing job. He "cleaned up" the school inside and out. Henry also replaced fourteen teachers and completed his assignment. Edenvale had turned the corner and was in far better shape. Understandably, during his tenure, Henry had made many enemies on the staff. Both Henry and the superintendent knew it was time for him to leave. Henry had set the stage for the next principal.

Now was the right time to bring in a new principal with a different set of skills, someone who knew curriculum and instruction. In 1988, after three frustrating years as the assistant superintendent in another district, I resigned. In fact, both the superintendent and I resigned on the same day.

That summer, I was fortunate to be rehired by Oak Grove School District once again as a principal. I did take a $20,000 reduction in salary. However, to say that I was delighted to return to Oak Grove was an understatement. I was so looking forward to becoming a principal once again. I was shocked when the superintendent assigned me to Edenvale School.

The superintendent gave me an assignment. "Henry set the stage for you. Your assignment is to develop a solid and cohesive K-6 instructional program, solidify the staff, and increase student achievement."

With that directive, I began my tenure at Edenvale School. The next nine years were the most rewarding years of my career.

Hi, Mom! Hi, Dad!

Creating a positive school environment...

On the first day at Edenvale School, I noticed something a little peculiar. When a parent came into the office, they were warmly greeted with a smile and a "Hi, Mom" or Hi, Dad." Both Julie, the school secretary, and Nancy, the health clerk, greeted parents the same way, "Hi, Mom" or "Hi, Dad."

After several days of hearing the same greeting to every parent, curiosity got the best of me. "Why do you greet every person who comes into the office with 'Hi, Mom' or 'Hi, Dad'?" The answer astounded me.

"Parents in this community want something better for their children. Most families are poor. Many parents work two or three jobs just to pay the rent and put food on the table. Some parents work at stores. Many are laborers, gardeners, caregivers, housecleaners. Edenvale is not about what parents do to put food on the table. Edenvale is all about the kids."

"Hi, Mom" or "Hi, Dad" put everyone on a level playing field. As parents realized and believed that we were only at Edenvale to teach their children, mistrust subsided. School was no longer seen as an enemy that had to be endured but more as a partner in helping children become the best they can be. Edenvale was a welcoming place for both students and parents and was on its way of becoming the focal point for the community.

All of this may sound hokey. So what! What rings true is that good things happen when "everyone is treated with dignity and respect...no matter what!"

Life Lesson: Making sure parents were never judged was important. When parents knew we were there only for their children, they became amazingly supportive. "Hi, Mom" or "Hi, Dad" put the emphasis just where it belonged...on kids!

Not Feeling Well

(Julie Fox, School Secretary)

Not long after the school year started, a new kindergartner came into the office. Tony said to me, "I don't feel so well."

"Let's go into the health office and see if we can find out what's wrong." Tony took my hand, and we walked together a few feet to the health office.

As Tony stood near the cot, I said, "I need to take your temperature to see if you have a fever." I turned to get a thermometer. When I turned back, Tony had his pants and underpants down around his ankles and was bent over the cot with his bottom up.

"Oh no, sweetie! Not that way!"

Note: You may only see the humor if you are old enough to remember rectal thermometers.

Saturday Is Paint Day

Creating a positive school environment...

The previous principal had done a great job restaffing and cleaning up the inside of the school. One problem, however, kept reoccurring...tagging. The building was tagged by gang members at least once a week, sometimes several times. In response, rival gang members would tag back. Tagging is about turf. Staff and parents really hated the constant tagging of the school.

One night, at a Parent Faculty Association meeting, the topic of tagging came up. "Why aren't the tags painted over immediately?" It was a good question.

In a large school district, it would sometimes take the maintenance department several days or weeks to paint over tags. In the meantime, the number of tags would grow. How could we "get ahead of the ongoing turf war?" Exasperated, one of the dads said, "Hell, if that is the case, give us some damn paint and we will paint over the graffiti."

His answer to the problem was a good one but was easier said than done. There were concerns by the district office. There were union contract conflicts. There were questions about another idea by this "crazy principal." To my benefit, district officials and union officials really talked about the problem and my request for paint. Both sides put the needs of the kids before their own turf concerns. We soon received several gallon buckets of the right color paint. In addition, paint rollers and cleanup materials were sent along.

At the next Parent Faculty Association meeting, a signup sheet was passed around and a phone tree set up. When the school was tagged, a phone call went out Friday afternoon. At nine o'clock on Saturday morning, six to ten parents would suddenly appear at the school, and within an hour or two, the graffiti was gone.

Saturday paint day became a regular part of school activities. We started noticing teenagers in the farthest corner of the schoolyard. Week after week, they just hung around and watched us. Apparently some of the volunteer painters were neighbors or parents of these teenagers. As soon as tags would appear, they would be painted over by parents. Gradually, the number of tags decreased, and within a year, the school was rarely tagged.

Life Lesson: Taking positive action is far more visible and effective than complaining.

Making a Deal with Gangs

Creating a positive school environment...

Graffiti was one issue. Gang members on campus during school were a different issue, a potentially dangerous one. I knew there was no way the gang culture was going to be eliminated in the neighborhood. At the time, many neighborhood teens did not have a lot of hope for a future. Forty-three percent dropped out of high school. Becoming part of a gang was a sign of being accepted, of belonging to something important.

The first couple of years, getting to know parents and people living in the Edenvale neighborhood was high priority for me. Although I am white, I grew up in poverty, poverty similar to the kind around Edenvale. I had been brought up to accept people for who they are and not make a lot of judgments about other people. Saturday mornings were spent walking around the neighborhood meeting people and introducing myself. I guess no principal had ever done that.

My Saturday morning walks were puzzling to many people, especially teenagers, but it was soon accepted that this was one of the things the new principal did. Mutual respect slowly developed. I wasn't seen as a threat to them or the neighborhood. "This guy is for real...he really cares about our kids and the neighborhood."

One day, toward the end of the school day, a message came into the office. "A bunch of gang members are on the playground." I had no idea of what to expect. Was there going to be a big problem? Had rival gangs set up a fight?

As I walked onto the playground, I recognized a couple of the gang members, and they recognized me. Of all things, they were playing basketball. Treating them with respect, I greeted them and asked if I could talk with them for a minute or two. "I am glad you are using the schoolyard and like playing basketball. I do need a little bit of your help." These teenage gang members were not sure what to think, but they were listening.

"I want you to feel free to play basketball at Edenvale as well as make use of the entire playground. Here's my problem. Under the California Education Code, nonstudents may not be on campus before the end of the school day. School is over at 3:00 p.m. every day. Would you guys be willing to wait on the sidewalk until the final bell rings? Then you are welcome to come on campus to play basketball."

The guys looked at me with a puzzled look. These gang members had expected to be hassled and were not expecting to hear what I said. They were not expecting to be treated with respect. They looked at one another. They shrugged. "OK."

After that, I frequently saw four or five gang members; they were becoming more and more like regular teenagers to me, standing on the sidewalk just before the end of the school day.

Over the next few months, some of the gang members and I had quite a few casual conversations. One day, I asked if they had little brothers and sisters attending Edenvale. The answer was yes, and they said they also had nieces and nephews attending Edenvale. I asked if they were ever concerned of the little kids' safety or if they might get hurt. All of them nodded their heads.

"You guys are older and making decisions for yourselves. Your decisions are fine with me," I said. "I just want the school to be a safe place for every little kid, whether or not an older brother belongs to a gang or to which gang." What I said made sense. Safety of their little brothers and sisters was something really important to them too.

It took some time and quite a few conversations with the members of both gangs, but Edenvale School became neutral turf. Edenvale became a safe place for every little sister or brother and every niece or nephew. The school did not belong to any gang; it belonged to the community. That basic agreement was still in effect when I left after nine years.

Life Lesson: When we are quick to judge people who appear different, we run many risks. We also miss many opportunities for understanding and the common good.

No Respect, No Headlights

Creating a positive school environment...

Becoming a neutral zone for gang activity obviously had a lot advantages for Edenvale School.

- Gang members dealt with their issues away from the school.
- Little kids were safer.
- The playground was used by lots of teenagers...not often at the same time.
- Graffiti was reduced to almost nothing. If someone new moved into the neighborhood and tagged the school, they got the word fast.

The idea of *respect* is paramount in the Hispanic community. Unfortunately, the Anglo community does not often see the importance of respect in the same way. It is our loss.

The respect that existed between gang members and Edenvale School was something that was not taken for granted. Both groups were very aware of the importance of *respect* in keeping the school safe for everyone's little brothers and sisters, waiting to come on campus until the final bell actually worked very well. However, nothing is ever perfect.

The night custodian had been at Edenvale for a number of years. He worked hard to keep the school clean and had a good relationship with neighborhood kids. One day, he called in sick, and a substitute named Alec was sent to cover his shift.

Alec was in his mid-twenties and apparently thought he was God's gift. Several hours after school was out, he had collected all the trash from classrooms and was taking it to the dumpster. He saw the older teens playing basketball. Although they were just playing basketball, Alec did not like their looks or think they should be on school grounds. Alec went over and hassled them. He didn't take time to listen to anything they said. To say the substitute custodian was disrespectful would be an understatement. The gang members had had enough and left.

Several hours later, when Alec had finished, it was time for him to leave and go home. Someone had taken a baseball bat and smashed his headlights. Alec was furious and demanded the person be caught and punished. Funny, no one was ever identified. *I also didn't look very hard.* Smashing headlights was not the right thing to do…however, "No respect! No headlights!"

> *Life Lesson: Treat everyone with dignity and respect. Respect means respect!*

2:00 a.m. Domestic Violence

*Sometimes something happens that just sticks
in my head. This anecdote is one.*

Creating a positive school environment...

Donna was an intern studying to get her school administrator credential. Donna would be at Edenvale on Mondays, Wednesdays, and
Fridays. Donna was also a San Jose Police Officer. She worked the
graveyard shift. It was purely coincidental that Donna's beat included
the Edenvale neighborhood. One of the good things about Donna's
internship was that she was able to see students and parents in two
different settings, which helped her see and understand kids a little
differently.

One Friday, Donna was late...about an hour late. When she got
to the school, she checked into the office and immediately went to
the classrooms. Usually, Donna would check in and we would talk
about plans for the day and what had happened since her last internship day. On this day, Donna's behavior was not typical. About a half

hour later, Donna returned to the office and we sat down. She had a relieved look on her face.

Donna told me the following story. "I received a domestic violence call about two this morning. Two officers responded. The father had hit the mother a number of times, and there was blood. As soon as the situation was stable, the father was handcuffed. I talked with the mother and the children. The mother was not seriously injured, and I had to determine if the children needed to be taken to the shelter." Donna said she determined it was safe for the children to stay with the mother, and the father was transported to jail.

Although I was well aware of domestic violence, this was the first time an incident had been directly shared with me. Donna told me that domestic violence calls in the middle of the night are not uncommon, especially on the weekends when there is a greater chance of alcohol being involved.

Donna told me, "The reason I went directly to the classroom was to check to see if the children were in school and were OK." Donna taught me something I have never forgotten. As a result of this event, I promised myself to help create as many *positive memories* as possible for kids attending Edenvale Elementary School.

Life Lesson: For many kids, school is the safest place they have…and kids want to feel safe.

Bumper Stickers

Creating a positive school environment...

Developing a strong instructional program and increasing student achievement were part of the assignment the superintendent gave me when I was assigned to Edenvale. Increasing student achievement required students to be directly and actively involved in both learning and the school. Edenvale could no longer be a place that allowed youngsters to passively sit in chairs. Students had to have a stake in the school. In a neighborhood that had "dropped out," getting youngsters to "buy in" was not easy. To get buy-in required a number of different approaches, each appealing to different youngsters. No single approach to getting buy-in would be enough.

Barbara, my wife, taught first-grade students. Attending educational conferences each year was one way for her to stay current and become a better teacher each year. In 1988, Barbara came home from a conference very excited. "I saw something I have never seen before. I saw a car with a bumper sticker that said 'My child was Student of the Month at _____ School." Neither of us had ever seen a "Student of the Month" bumper sticker.

What an idea! What a way to make students to buy in...being acknowledged on a bumper sticker that was on Mom's car. What a way for a parent to say, "I am proud of my child and what he/she is accomplishing in school." What a visible way to help change the public image of Edenvale! "My Child Is Student of the Month at Edenvale School" bumper stickers were immediately ordered.

As soon as I ordered the "Student of the Month" bumper stickers, I realized there was a problem. Only about 200 youngsters would receive bumper stickers in a year. Two hundred was simply too few to dramatically create a new public image at Edenvale. A second order was placed. By adding a second bumper sticker for "Student of the Week," we increased the number to 720. With the addition of "Student of the Week," every student had a genuine opportunity to be publicly acknowledged by his/her teacher.

It worked! Edenvale had the only bumper sticker in town. In the first two months, about 200 bumper stickers were awarded. When we started seeing "Edenvale" bumper stickers on cars all over Santa Clara County, we were amazed and pleased. Edenvale had started something new and positive. Within a few weeks, we started to receive inquiries from other schools. Soon we started seeing bumper stickers from many other schools.

Receiving a "Student of the Month" or "Student of the Week" bumper sticker was a big deal for students. However, seeing their own "Student of the Week" or "Student of the Month" bumper sticker on their parents' car was the biggest deal of all.

Life Lesson: Be sure to give thanks when someone shares a great idea.

Pimps, Prostitutes,
and Drug Dealers

New Year's Eve...

Perhaps it was the way parents were welcomed to Edenvale when they came into the office. Perhaps it was all the Saturday mornings I walked around the neighborhood meeting people. Perhaps it was that parents no longer saw the school as a place they had to send their children to. Perhaps it was that more and more parents felt they were a part of the school. Perhaps it was "Hi, Mom" or "Hi, Dad." I am not really sure.

I do know that many new staff members really believed that they had the ability to make a difference in the lives of each of their students. Edenvale was focused on children to help them develop the skills needed to be successful in school and successful in life. What was happening at Edenvale was not lip service to an ideal. Although staff and I were always striving to be better, what was happening at Edenvale was the real deal. The school was now the centerpiece of the neighborhood rather than a place where parents had to send their children to.

As the principal and educational leader of the community, my job was to provide a solid education for every child academically, socially, and emotionally, not to make judgments about parents or the kind of work they engaged in. If an adult was engaged in something illegal, it was a police issue, *not* a school issue.

Meeting parents in the neighborhood on Saturday mornings and making them feel welcome at school was a game changer. People in the neighborhood became less guarded. I liked the neighborhood and the people I met during my tenure. Although I never asked about the kind of work they did, I learned a great deal about the challenges of having minimum-wage jobs. Parents often worked two or three jobs just to pay the rent and put food on the table. Over time, I came to know that some parents had unconventional jobs. There were a couple of pimps, a few prostitutes, and several drug dealers. I learned that almost all of the parents were doing their best to provide for their children. That alone was good enough for me; I learned not to judge parents and just focus on students.

Then something happened. On New Year's Eve, we had made dinner reservations at the Fairmont Hotel in San Jose. Going to a fancy restaurant was not something we did very often, but this was New Year's Eve.

After parking the car, we walked in a side entrance to the hotel on our way to the restaurant. Unexpectedly, I heard, "Mr. Smith. Hi, Mr. Smith!" We turned and there were two Edenvale parents, Sandy and Carol. I had met these caring moms a number of times and knew their children well. Both moms had great personalities and easy smiles.

We chatted and I introduced Barbara, my wife. Then Sandy said, "We have a room upstairs. Come on up and have a drink to celebrate the New Year." It was a tempting offer. We did have a few minutes before our dinner reservation. Barbara was surprised when I politely turned down their offer. Sandy asked again, and I said, "Thanks, but we have a dinner reservation that we need to keep. Have a wonderful New Year's Eve."

With that, we walked down the hall toward the restaurant. Barbara was scowling; I could tell she was very upset with me. "How could you? It was such a thoughtful invitation by two of your Edenvale parents. I cannot imagine you being that rude." Barbara was more than upset...she was pissed off.

Just before we arrived at the restaurant, there was little alcove. I stopped and pulled Barbara aside. "I need to explain something to you. Both Sandy and Carol have children going to school at Edenvale.

"They are good moms and very nice people. The little girl is in second grade and the little boy is in kindergarten." Barbara just nodded. "These attractive Edenvale moms are not here by accident. They have a room upstairs. They have plenty of booze." Barbara looked puzzled. "Sandy and Carol are here tonight to make money, hopefully quite a lot of money. They are here working. They are prostitutes."

Over the years, both as a principal and assistant superintendent, I have appeared in articles published by the San Jose Mercury more times than I would have liked. Rarely are school administrators in the newspaper for good news. Usually we are in the newspaper because there is a *big* problem.

"Although it would be OK to have a drink with Sandy and Carol, this is the Fairmont Hotel. This is New Year's Eve. There are many people here, and a few may know who I am even if I don't know them. What would happen if I was seen coming out a prostitute's room? What would happen if a story appeared in the San Jose Mercury?" Barbara and I then went into the restaurant and had a lovely New Year's Eve dinner.

Life Lesson: Once in a while, it is better when I do not do what my wife would like.

Green Tickets

Creating a positive school environment...

As parents, we often "catch our kids when they do something wrong." Traditionally, the same thing is true in schools. However, if we want to change kids' attitudes from dropping out to staying in, a different approach is needed. How about focusing on catching kids doing something right?

The "green ticket" idea was born. Green tickets were given out in the classroom, at recess, in the cafeteria—anywhere a staff member saw something positive and wanted to acknowledge a student.

Green tickets were small, one-fourth the size of a regular piece of paper. They were preprinted as a pad with a place for a name, date, teacher's name, signature, and a list of fourteen behaviors for which we were looking. There was also a blank space to write in something that was observed and was not included on the list. The green tickets were glued together like a tablet so they could easily be torn off and given to a child.

It took just a second for a staff member to put a check next to one of the fourteen items, sign it, and give it to the student. A student could not ask for a green ticket. They had to be caught by a staff member! About a hundred green tickets were handed out each day.

Problem: what to do with the two thousand green tickets handed out each month? Idea: collect them. Put out two five-gallon buckets in front of the office, one for the primary grades and one for the upper grades. Students would be responsible for putting their own green tickets into the correct bucket.

Every time there was an assembly, draw six to ten green tickets. Give out a small prize such as a special pencil, eraser, or something else that would make a good school-related prize. It worked! What amazing student buy-in!

Life Lesson: Catching kids being good creates an environment in which more and more kids are doing the right thing.

Management vs Discipline

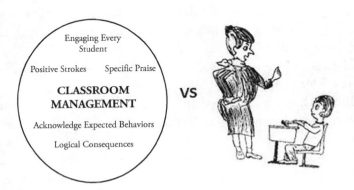

Creating a positive school environment...

When many of us attended school, we just assumed that what the teacher said was what you did. If you didn't do what the teacher said, you expected swift and strong discipline. If a teacher had several students in her classroom that frequently did not do what the teacher wanted, a lot of teaching time was spent on discipline...crime and punishment. Most teachers did not like it, and other students in the class didn't like wasting time, while a few students were reprimanded or punished. The cycle would go on day after day.

Could this cycle be short-circuited?

The idea behind *classroom discipline* is that a teacher *reacts* strongly after an incident happens. The teacher disciplines the student for doing something wrong. The teacher takes time and tries to correct what happened.

The idea behind *classroom management* is that a teacher acts in ways that *helps prevent* many incidents before they happen. If 70 to 80 percent of the incidents can be routinely prevented, the number of incidents requiring discipline is greatly reduced and the amount of time available for instruction is increased.

The title of this anecdote is "Management vs Discipline." The title was chosen to get your attention. A more correct title would be "Management and Discipline." A basic question is how does a teacher want to spend his/her time? There are specific techniques that teachers can use to minimize bad behavior that end up requiring the use of teaching time for discipline. In reality, teaching and learning are enhanced when discipline and management are combined as part of the everyday operation in a classroom.

Classroom management requires a teacher to refocus how he/she looks at students throughout a lesson. Is the teacher "just waiting for something to happen that interrupts the lesson," or is the teacher using positive student interaction techniques to increase student involvement in learning? The more students are actively involved in learning, the more they learn and the number of disruptive behaviors decreases.

Basic concept: everyone needs attention...we call them strokes. The number of strokes needed each day may vary significantly from person to person. Strokes help people feel worthwhile or valuable or at least get attention. To young children, how they get the number of strokes they need does not really matter; negative strokes and positive strokes all count toward the needed total for the day. Just think for a moment about two-year-olds and what happens with their behavior when they do not think they are getting the attention they want or deserve.

Focus on acknowledging the kind of behavior we want to see.

- Do we want to see students focused on learning rather than be distracted?
- Do we want to see students actively engaged in lessons?
- Do we want to see students asking questions?
- Do we want to see students putting forth their best effort?
- Do we want to see students being kind and considerate to others?
- Do we want to manage student behavior in a way that short-circuits most problems before they occur?

Classroom management is a set of skills, a set of skills that can be learned and then practiced on a daily basis.

- Constantly move around the classroom as you teach; resist being the "sage on the stage."
    - When a teacher is moving around the classroom, the teacher creates physical proximity to many more students, and it becomes easier to make one-on-one contact and easier to see what students are doing.
    - The teacher also has many more opportunities to quietly acknowledge students when they do something well or are behaving appropriately.
    - The teacher has more opportunities to see early if a student is having trouble understanding a concept and take immediate steps to clarify or reteach.

- Engaging students is an easy way to give positive strokes in front of the whole class.
    - "David, what do you think the next step will be?"
    - "This side of the class is really focused on completing the assignment."
    - "Anna, what do you think is next?"
    - "Sam, that is a very good question. Who thinks they can answer Sam's question?"

- Engaging students is an easy way to give positive strokes to individuals.
    - "Pedro, you are really thinking about what you are doing."
    - "I like the way you are paying attention."
    - "Nice work!"
    - "Good Job!"

- Engaging students is an easy way to create opportunists to give positive strokes to students with a high potential of being disruptive.

- Alex has a high potential of being disruptive. John sits next to Alex. Alex is off task. Instead of engaging Alex, engage John.

  - "John, I can see that you really got to work when I gave you the worksheet." Alex will notice that the teacher gives John a stroke.

  - As soon as the teacher sees Alex behaving as expected, the teacher gives Alex a stroke. "I like the way you got to work."

  - When Alex realizes he/she is more likely to get a stroke by doing the right thing, the more frequently Alex will engage in positive rather than disruptive behavior.

  - Work on catching Alex engaging in the kinds of behaviors wanted. Over time, Alex is likely to make an effort to get positive strokes and fewer efforts to get strokes by misbehaving.

  - This approach works with most students over time. How much easier it is to make a quick positive statement than it is to stop a lesson and discipline a student?

- Is this approach magic? Will it stop all disruptive behavior? No!
  - Nothing works all the time.
  - Think of it this way:

A gift for you

Enjoy your gift! From alysha

amazon Gift Receipt

Send a Thank You Note

You can learn more about your gift or start a return here too.

Scan using the Amazon app or visit **https://a.co/cvbtVa4**

Ask Assia, Vani A Nepal

- In a poker game, you are dealt a hand with a pair of fours. How much are you going to wager on a pair of fours?
- You are dealt with a full house. How much are you going to wager on a full house?
- With either hand, you can win or lose. What are the odds?
- Would you rather bet on a hand with an 80 percent chance of winning or on a hand with a 20 percent chance?

- Classroom management is like an 80 percent poker hand. I'll take those odds anytime.

Think about one or two of your most favorite teachers. Why did you like them so much? Was it the subject matter? Was it the manner in which the material was presented? Was it how your favorite teacher treated you and other students? Was it their skill at disciplining students, or was it their skill in managing the students in the classroom?

Over the years, I have taught many classroom management workshops. This explanation of classroom management is meant to be just a short introduction to the topic.

Life Lesson: Some people think that teaching is an art. Other people think it is a science. It's probably both. However, even an artist with a lot of natural talent takes lessons to develop new techniques and skills. Artists are lifelong learners. Good teachers are also lifelong learners.

Cleanest School

TRASH   BUCKETS

Creating a positive school environment…

Youngsters do make mistakes. Kids do misbehave. Students are sent to the principal's office. These are just facts of life in a school. Traditionally, kids are benched at recess or lunch or given lines to write over and over for small infractions. However, how a principal handles these everyday situations depends on how a principal views youngsters.

Two principles guided me when working with youngsters on a day-to-day basis: "catch them being good" and "use logical consequences" when they are not. Benching kids or having them write lines were senseless punishments…nothing positive about them, just punishments.

I thought about kids sitting on the bench during recess and lunch. Often the thing that got a kid benched was excess energy in class. Just sitting on a bench certainly did nothing to get rid of the excess energy. One day, I walked outside to be sure the kids were sitting on the bench in front of the office. Sure enough, three kids were sitting on the bench with their legs swinging back and forth in sheer boredom. I also saw the green ticket buckets in front of the office.

Was there a way for kids to get rid of some of the excess energy in a positive way? Was there a way to create a logical consequence to everyday kinds of misbehavior and help change the school's image at the same time?

The next time a student was benched, I came out of the office with a five-gallon bucket labeled "Clean School Bucket." "Instead of sitting on the bench, you are to fill up this bucket with trash you find around the school. When lunch hour is over, bring the bucket back to the office. It must be at least half full."

After a few weeks, the buckets had fewer pieces of trash—papers, cups, or other discarded items, and more and more twigs and fallen leaves. A year later, Edenvale won a contest sponsored by the City of San Jose. We proudly flew the "Cleanest School in San Jose" flag along with the American flag and the California State flag for the next school year.

Life Lesson: When we slow down, we can often find alternative ways of solving problems that may be far more positive than a more traditional approach.

Drill: Shooter on Campus

Creating a positive school environment...

This event happened ten years before the Columbine High School massacre in which thirteen were killed and twenty-one were injured.

In January 1989, I had been the principal at Edenvale Elementary School only a few months. An incident in nearby Stockton, California, shook me to my core.

A gunman came on the schoolyard at Cleveland Elementary School, a school with similar student demographics to Edenvale. Within four minutes, the gunman had fired 106 rounds, killing five and injuring thirty-two children. His victims were predominately Southeast Asian refugees. His weapon of choice was an AK-47.

If it could happen in Stockton, it could happen in San Jose. It could also happen at Edenvale.

To be sure, there had been school shootings before. In the decade of the 1950s, there were sixteen shootings at schools with thirteen deaths in the United States. In the 1970s, there were twenty-nine school shootings with thirty-seven deaths. Most often the weapon of choice was a pistol or a revolver. It wasn't until the late 1980s that assault rifles started becoming the weapon of choice. The use of assault rifles resulted in mass shootings, with large numbers of dead and injured.

The mass shooting at Cleveland Elementary School was the first time I remember hearing that an assault rifle was used to kill young children. Five dead and thirty-two injured within four minutes. I just couldn't wrap my mind around what had happened or why. What could schools do? How could schools prepare for such an unthinkable act?

As far as I knew, in 1989, there were no protocols for school shootings. There were no code reds. There was no training available. There was no preparedness drill like there were for fires or earthquakes. Mass shootings at schools were still inconceivable.

Could we develop a drill for a shooter on the playground? In our discussions, honestly, the thought of a shooter coming inside an elementary school building *never* crossed my mind. Teachers and I talked. What would a possible drill look like? What might the characteristic of a shooter be like? For better or worse, the following is what we thought.

- A shooter would likely be male.
- A shooter would likely have some experience, but not a lot of experience, with weapons and how they react when fired.
- A shooter would likely have difficulty controlling the kick of a weapon, meaning the trajectory of rounds that tend to go slightly upward.
- If youngsters dropped to the ground and played dead, they might have a better chance of surviving.

The drill we created was not very sophisticated. However, we thought it might reduce the number of youngsters killed or injured in a real event. (I still do not know if our assumptions were valid.)

We decided to try the "shooter on campus" drill at recess with the fourth-, fifth-, and sixth-grade students. Teachers talked with their students over several days about the idea of having this kind of drill and what students would need to do to keep them safe. The message was, "Drop and play dead. Do not move. Play dead on the ground until an announcement is made from the office that the drill is over." This idea of a "shooter on campus" drill was definitely an experiment.

On the day of the "shooter on campus" drill, I put on a long tan-colored raincoat and concealed a broom with a black handle under the raincoat. After walking onto the middle of the playground, I opened the raincoat and pulled out the broom. Holding it up like a rifle and pointing it in the directions of the students, I yelled, "Boom! Boom!" Each time the broom rifle was pointed in another direction, I yelled, "Boom! Boom!" By the third "Boom! Boom!" every student was lying flat on the ground and playing dead. No one moved as I continued to point in different directions and yelled, "Boom! Boom!"

After a few minutes, I put the broom rifle back under the raincoat and then left the playground. Students did not move. They stayed on the ground and continued to play dead. Back at the office, I made the announcement that the drill was over. I thanked the students for knowing what to do. I let them know they had done a very good job at playing dead. I do not remember doing another drill.

I do not remember hearing about mass shootings at schools for the next several years…until Columbine ten years later. Columbine shocked the nation. After Columbine, police departments and school district worked feverishly to develop detailed protocols, including code red. However, mass shootings have continued year in and year out. There is always a lot of talk and prayers after each school shooting but little, if any, action. Over three hundred mass shootings took place in 2018.

After the tragic mass shooting at Parkland High School, I wrote a message to everyone who is in the Adopt-A-College program Facebook group. I shared my horror that mass killings in school were still taking place almost twenty years after Columbine and that nothing had really been done to stop mass school shootings. I shared that I thought the bright and articulate survivors of Parkland may be the best hope for sensible legislation. I mentioned the "shooter on campus" drill that we did at Edenvale in 1989…almost thirty years ago. I was shocked by the number of former students who posted that they vividly remember the "shooter on campus" drill. I am shocked that the "shooter on campus" drill made such a lasting impact. I am even more shocked that twenty years after Columbine, nothing has really been done in response to these horrific shootings. Prayers and talk, yes! Action, *no*!

Life Lesson: I do not know what the life lesson is for this anecdote. I can only hope that somehow our society can find a way to have honest dialogue, find common ground, and enact some kind of common-sense legislation for military-style assault weapons. Children, who are simply attending school, have done nothing to warrant being massacred.

Shin Guards, Anyone?

Jamie was a feisty third grader. Although she liked school and her teacher, Jamie had a mind of her own. Her teacher, Mr. C, was introducing cursive writing to the class. Jamie did not want to learn cursive writing; printing was just fine by her. When it came time for a cursive writing lesson, Jamie would throw a literal fit, disrupting the entire class. Mr. C and I tried a number of strategies; they all failed. Then Jamie refused to go to class at all.

Jamie's mother and I had a long conference. I needed to understand what was going on in Jamie's head; her mother wanted to know too! We were both puzzled. Finally we agreed that it was probably that Jamie had just made up her mind that she was not going to learn cursive, and that was the end of the story.

Both of us agreed that Jamie had to be in school, not necessarily in class but in school. We came up with a plan. Mom would dress Jamie in sweat clothes just in case she became belligerent. Mom would drive Jamie to school, and I would meet them at the curbside drop-off. We would make it clear that Jamie was going to be in school. She could either go to class or spend the day in the health office. If Jamie refused to go to class, Mom and I would escort Jamie to the health office to spend the day on the cot or until she changed her mind.

We had a plan and we were ready…or so we thought.

Mom brought Jamie to school. I met them in the parking lot. I gave Jamie a choice of going to class or spending the day in the health office. Mom opened the car door. Jamie refused to get out of the car. Mom and I repeated the choices. Jamie still refused to get out of the car. Mom and I lifted her out of the seat to take her to the health office.

Immediate pain shot down my calf and shin. I had no idea what had happened. I limped as we escorted Jamie to the health office. When we put Jamie on the cot in the health office, I realized what had happened. Mom made sure Jamie was wearing sweat clothes; however, I had not said anything about wearing sneakers. Jamie had on Mary Janes and, with all her might, had scraped through my pant leg, down my calf and shin. It took several days for the scrapes and bruises to heal.

Life Lesson: When developing a plan, be sure to think about the details.

Peeing on the Window

The Edenvale neighborhood is a tough place in which to grow up.

The start of each new school year at Edenvale Elementary School was exciting. I was always full of energy and had a hard time sleeping the night before. I eagerly looked forward to greeting youngsters from last year and meeting the new students.

The formal welcome for the year occurred at a short assembly during the first few days. One year, the assembly was on the third day of school. Kindergarten through third-grade students gathered in the cafeteria early in the school day, followed by fourth- through sixth-grade students after the morning recess. Each assembly was short and only lasted about fifteen or twenty minutes.

This assembly was important because it allowed me to set the stage and expectations for the year. I started by welcoming new students to Edenvale. I asked all the new students to raise their hands so that everyone could see how many new students there were. (Since the community has lots of low-income apartments, the school had quite a high student mobility rate—between 40 percent and 50 percent.) I always made a special effort to welcome all the new students.

I then asked the returning students to raise their hands. I welcomed them and told them how glad I was that they had returned to Edenvale for another year. Next, I talked about the responsibility of all returning students to help the new students learn the way we do things at Edenvale and the way we treat each other. We called it the Edenvale Way.

I talked, in some detail, about how each student is expected to behave and how that behavior looks to others. Behavior at Edenvale is still based upon four simple ideas.

- I am safe.
- I treat everyone with respect.
- I am courteous.
- I am doing my personal best.

Out of the corner of my eye, I noticed the body language of a new upper-grade student. He was definitely not having any of this Edenvale Way bullshit. As I talked, I scanned the audience and made eye contact with as many youngsters as possible. This practice was really important in setting the stage for the year. However, my eye kept coming back to this one particular new student. We made eye contact for a moment. He looked at me, and I looked at him. Although he said nothing, his look was defiant. I later found out his name was Roberto and that he was a new fifth grader.

Roberto transferred from a tough school, and he thought he was really tough. He thought he knew a lot, but after just three days, Roberto did not know much about the difference between the lower-grade and upper-grade schedules or much of anything else about Edenvale. Apparently, Roberto had decided at the assembly that he was going to find a way show us what he thought of this school and its Edenvale Way.

Edenvale School was built in the 1960s and is made up of four very large round buildings that are connected by restrooms and major doorways. Between the cafeteria pod and the yard, there was a walkway that curved around the building. Since the walkway curved, about thirty feet of the walkway was hard to see or supervise.

Somehow Roberto realized he was unsupervised for this short distance. There was a small alcove with a classroom door and dark-tinted window. Roberto had the brilliant idea of graphically demonstrating how he felt about his new school. He stepped into the alcove, unzipped his pants, and proceeded to urinate all over the window. In total defiance, he said, "I will show you, Edenvale. This is what I think about you and the Edenvale Way!"

As I said, Roberto did not know much about how the school functioned. He was unaware that the primary youngsters had lunch first and were back in class by the time upper-grade youngsters finished lunch and walked to the playground. Roberto was unaware that he was peeing on the dark-tinted window of a primary classroom. The students were already back in class. He was also unaware that the large classroom chalkboard was next to the tinted window. Naturally, student desks faced the chalkboard. Since Roberto could not see into the classroom, it was not obvious to this new fifth grader that thirty second graders watched his prolonged urination performance.

News travels fast, even at an elementary school. By the time school was out, most youngsters and almost every teacher knew about Roberto's stunt. Everyone knew and laughed. Robert was mortified and humiliated—a logical consequence resulting from his own actions. I guess the result was a good example of an unintended consequence, or one might say, an example of the Edenvale Way.

The next day, I saw Roberto on the playground and walked up to him. He knew that I knew. I shook his hand with a firm grip, looked him in the eye, and said, "I see you started learning about the Edenvale Way yesterday during lunch recess." Apparently, Roberto got the message. Amazingly, for the rest of the year, I never saw him for disciplinary reasons. Roberto wasn't really as tough as he thought he was.

Life Lesson: Sometimes logical consequences and judgment from peers is far more severe than any punishment by the principal could be.

Girls at War!

Sixth-grade girls can be a challenge. They can be sweet and considerate, and they can be bitchy, nasty, and vindictive.

John Bowlin was a well-loved teacher; by students, other teachers, and parents. He was a natural teacher. John's lessons were interesting and fun. Students frequently worked together on projects. Youngsters were really motivated to learn. Rarely did John have a discipline issue that he could not handle.

One lunchtime, John stopped by my office. Rarely did John ask for advice, but today was different. "I do not know what to do," he said. "I have two girls in my class who are at each other all the time, both in class and on the playground. Maria and Carmen are constantly mean to each other. Both girls make up lies about the other and tell their friends the lies. Often they get their friends involved

111

in being mean too. The hostility between them is so great that they frequently disrupt classroom learning. Something has to be done!"

Wow! John really unloaded, and I knew he was at his wits' end. I also knew I had to do something and do it that day. For John's sake, I could not wait until tomorrow. I had seen this kind of petty and vindictive behavior between girls before. I also knew the behavior was difficult to control. I needed time to think, but action was needed now. What would logical consequences look like?

"John, do not be surprised when I open the door to your classroom after lunch."

When I knew the students had settled in after lunch and John was teaching a lesson, I quietly opened his door. "Mr. Bowlin, may I please see Maria and Carmen in the hall for a moment?" Both girls followed me into the hallway, and I closed the door behind them. They looked at each other with disdain.

"Maria and Carmen, there is a problem that has to be solved. I know both of you hate each other, I understand that." I paused and then continued, "I know that you go out of your way to be mean to each other and to involve you friends in being mean too. The way you treat each other has to stop!" After pausing again, I continued, "Either you solve the problem or I will solve the problem. It does not matter to me which way the problem is solved, but it will be solved."

Maria and Carmen looked at me, wondering what I meant, but I had their attention.

"I do not expect you to like each other. I certainly do not expect you to ever become friends. That would be unrealistic, if not impossible. I do expect the way you are treating each other stops now and stops for the rest of the year. I expect you to treat each other with respect." I saw smirks on their faces. "What does Mr. Smith think? Respect? No way! Mr. Smith just doesn't get it."

There was a long pause. I repeated, "Either you two figure out how to solve your problem with each other, or I will solve it. It does not matter to me which way the problem gets solved. The problem will get solved. How is totally up to you." Both girls looked puzzled... *What does he mean it is totally up to us? How is Mr. Smith going to make us change? How will he discipline or punish us? Whatever he does, it won't change anything between us.*

Maintaining my usual calm yet sincere voice, I said, "If you will not solve the problem, you need to know the way I will solve it. You will be transferred to another school." A slight grin appeared on each girl's face, as each thought the other would be transferred and she would be the one to get to stay in Mr. Bowlin's class.

Their reaction is just what I had hoped to see. After another pause, I continued, "I will transfer you to another school. You will be out of Mr. Bowlin's class and out of Edenvale School. Let me be clear, I will transfer *both* of you to different schools…not one of you but *both* of you." I could see disbelief in their eyes… *Mr. Smith would send both of us to different schools?*

"The choice is totally up to you. If you choose to make peace with each other, you will both stay in Mr. Bowlin's class. However, if you continue the way you currently treat each other, I will transfer *both* of you immediately. Do you understand, really understand?" I was not looking for an answer nor expecting an answer.

We stood silently in the hallway for a minute. Finally, I said, "The choice is up to you. Both of you need think about the two choices and figure it out. I will know your choice by what you do and how you treat each other." I opened the door to Mr. Bowlin's classroom. "Now it is time to go back to class." I closed the door behind them and wondered what would happen. To this day, I do not know how Carmen and Maria managed it, but both finished sixth grade at Edenvale School.

Life Lesson: From Carmen and Maria, I learned that when the desire for something is big enough (such as the desire to stay in Mr. Bowlin's class), a way can usually be found to accomplish it.

I'll Trade You Toilet Paper
for Paper Towels

Surviving hard times...

The decades of the 1980s and 1990s were often financially tough for school districts. Year after year, districts would have to cut or eliminate programs to balance the budget. As Director of Instruction and as an assistant superintendent, I was one of the district officials tasked with coming up with a million-dollar cut one year, a three million-dollar cut a couple of years later, followed by another two-million-dollar cut, and so on. Music and art were often the first areas cut, while athletics were seldom reduced. Those years were awful! The hardest times were when it was necessary to increase class size and lay off teachers.

Curriculum and instruction were my areas of expertise. Three times in my career, I had wonderful experiences developing programs and creating opportunities for children. Going to work each day was exciting and fun.

In contrast, I was involved in reducing or eliminating programs twice within ten years. It was painful, very painful. The third time massive program cuts were required, I retired. I just did not have the heart to once again be part of dismantling programs that were good for youngsters. A third time was more pain than I could endure.

A couple of years after I had returned to being a principal, I had to deal with reducing budgets on a school level. We had to ration duplication paper to one ream (five hundred sheets) per teacher per week. That's not much paper when you are a teacher and responsible for thirty students, six subject areas five days a week...just do the math.

That same year, things like pencils, cleaning supplies, play-ground balls, toilet paper, and paper towels were also rationed. At Back-to-School Night, many teachers came up with the idea of a classroom wish list. Many parents who could not really afford to went out and purchased pencils, crayons, Kleenex, and other things needed in classrooms. But what do you do when the school runs out of toilet paper?

Principals are nothing if not able to come up with creative solutions in difficult situations. We were running low on toilet paper. In the spring, I received a phone call from another principal. Bob was desperate for paper towels. He had extra toilet paper, and I had extra paper towels.

Fortunately, the year before, I had been able to convince the district to install electric hand dryers in student restrooms...if I could get them donated. By convincing a vendor to use Edenvale as a demonstration project, it would benefit both of us. Their donation paid off over and over again as school districts began to buy hand dryers. Edenvale was the first school to have electric hand dryers in student restrooms, hence the extra cases of paper towels.

Bob offered me a deal—five cases of toilet paper for four cases of paper towels. The deal was made, and we made it through the end of the year.

Life Lesson: When required, a school can cut back on many things...toilet paper is not one of them.

Condoms, Anyone?

One never knows when something unexpected is going to happen. I never conceived this anecdote could really happen at an elementary school.

It was springtime and a beautiful day. Jo Fukasawa had taught fifth grade for many years. She was a consummate teacher—subject matter, classroom management—and she really believed in her ability to make a positive difference in the lives of every one of her students. I do not remember Jo ever sending a student to the principal's office. She was just that good of a teacher. Edenvale Elementary School was truly blessed with many teachers like Jo Fukasawa.

Mrs. Fukasawa came into my office at lunchtime and she was distraught. In six years, I had never seen her rattled. This was a first!

I asked, "Jo, what on earth happened? What is wrong?" She could barely get the words out. "Andy," she stammered. "Andy, one of my students, is passing out condoms to the other boys...a dozen condoms. I don't know what to do!"

I tried to reassure her. "OK, Jo, we will figure this out." I thought long and hard. This was a first. Edenvale is an elementary school, not a junior high or high school. How should I handle this situation? What were my options? What should be the consequence for handing out condoms to other fifth- and six-grade boys? What would be a logical consequence? This situation was serious. I pondered each question.

Finally, I said, "As soon as lunch is over, send Andy to see me." A few minutes later, lunch ended and students had returned to their classrooms. Mrs. Fukasawa told Andy that the principal wanted to see him in the office.

Andy appeared at my door, and his face was ashen. He just knew he was in trouble...big trouble! I directed Andy to sit down in a chair next to me.

I spoke to Andy in a soft yet very stern voice. "Andy, you and I have a problem. I know that you gave condoms to some boys." Andy nodded. "Well, Andy, I want you to understand something. We do not do condoms at Edenvale School." (If I had been principal at a junior high school, I would have chosen very different words, but this was an elementary school.)

Continuing, I said, "You are in trouble. How much trouble depends upon you!" Not understanding, Andy looked at me with his eyes wide open. Obviously, he had no idea what was going to happen next.

"Andy, you know each of the boys to whom you gave a condom." Andy nodded his head. "You need to get all the condoms back. Lunch hour is over and you will have to go to each boy's classroom and ask him to give the condom back to you. Since all outside doors are locked, you will need to knock on each classroom door. When the monitor opens the door, you will politely ask the teacher if you may see each boy for a minute. Then you are to ask for the condom back. Do you understand?" Andy did not say a word but he nodded. Finally I said, "When you have collected all of the condoms, come back to the office and see me." Again, Andy nodded his head. He slowly walked out of my office, his shoulders slumping.

Andy was gone a long time, almost forty-five minutes. When he returned, his head hung down, and he looked very sad. I directed Andy to sit down and put the condoms on the table. He sadly shook his head from side to side; he was almost in tears. "Mr. Smith, I am sorry. I was only able to get eleven condoms back."

I looked at Andy sternly. After several seconds, I spoke. "Andy, I know you tried hard to get all the condoms back. You did get eleven out of twelve of them. What you did took a lot of effort. It also took courage to knock on each classroom door and ask each boy to give the condom back to you." After pausing for a long moment, I said, "I will accept the eleven condoms and that you completed the task I assigned you. You did your personal best, and I accept your personal best." I heard a little sigh of relief.

"Now we have one final problem so solve. I assume the box of condoms belongs to your father." Andy nodded. "I cannot let you take the condoms home. However, tell your dad that I have his box of condoms. He may stop by the office anytime and pick them up."

Andy's dad never did come by the office to pick up the condoms.

Life Lesson: Discipline based upon logical consequences is usually far more effective than discipline based upon punishment.

The Train Has Left!

Henry Castanada, the previous principal, had "cleaned up" Edenvale School. Many of the fourteen new teachers had heard the stories about Edenvale and were not thrilled about being transferred. All fourteen were good solid teachers. Some "begged" not to be sent to Edenvale. During the first couple of years as principal, a few more "reluctant dragons" left.

The school now had a majority of strong teachers. However, they taught as individuals, not as part of a team. My task was to start building a cohesive team. The task was far from easy.

At staff meetings, we often talked about instruction and what needed to happen to increase student achievement. It took a long time to get teachers to agree that they could be more effective if each grade level worked as a team. To create grade-level teams, I found a way for each team to spend a full day together each month, without students. The purpose was to work and plan together, resulting in a common curricular focus that would result in improved learning for all students. For me, the challenge was finding great substitute teachers and creating a consistent substitute team that would take over a grade level for one day each month.

Since Edenvale was a kindergarten through sixth grade, the team was on campus seven days each month. After a couple of months, the substitute team became familiar faces to students. The substitute teachers were accepted by students as just other staff members of Edenvale School. The team looked forward to being in the same classrooms each time. The students looked forward to the special lessons the teachers brought with them.

Planning days, or Integrated Thematic Instruction as I called it, were far more successful than I had hoped. The planning days allowed teachers to share ideas, write lesson plans together, share instructional techniques with each other, and develop a common focus for their grade level. Because each planning day was a full day without students, many team members developed strong professional relationships and lasting friendships. The cost of each planning day was about $750, well worth the development of strong, cohesive teams at each grade level. The planning days lasted about two years and then were no longer needed. Planning together became the norm, and staff found ways to work and plan together each week after school.

The success of planning days did not mean everything was perfect at Edenvale School. Although we had a staff of solid teachers, a few did not see the merit of planning together. Some teachers resisted the idea sharing their secrets of teaching. A few preferred to be rugged individualists and go their own way. In many schools, being a rugged individualist would be just fine; it is simply what not was needed coming out of the turbulent years at Edenvale School in the 1970s and 1980s.

Dede Clark transferred to Edenvale soon after I became principal. Dede was a good strong teacher but very unsure about where Edenvale was going and how we were getting there. Frequently, Dede pushed back in subtle and not-so-subtle ways. As a staff and school, we were making good progress by working together and focusing on developing a cohesive instructional program. After three years, Edenvale was well on its way, but Dede wasn't sure.

The school year ended, and there was a lot to think about. A challenge for me was what to do with Dede Clark. She definitely was a good teacher but she was not onboard. Dede's rugged individualist attitude had become a real dilemma. I did not want to force her to transfer to another school, but something had to change. Just before the start of the school year, I had an idea.

Staff members return to school about a week or so before the students. The first morning teachers returned, I usually left a personal note on each desk that welcomed them back. One year, I left a lemon on each teacher's desk and a note saying that Edenvale was "well on the way of changing lemons into lemonade."

I do not remember the content of the notes I left this particular year; however, I do vividly remember what I left on Dede's desk. I had found a little train during the summer. I left it on her desk with a note saying, "The Edenvale train has left the station. Are you on board or not?" Dede Clark stayed at Edenvale long after I had retired.

Each year, Adopt-A-College scholarships are awarded to graduating high school seniors who had attended Edenvale School and planned on continuing their education at a trade school, community college, or university. This year, Dede was retiring. On the front of the printed program was a paragraph honoring Dede for her service to the children and her love of Edenvale School. Dede was the very last person left at Edenvale who was a teacher when I was a principal.

During the event, Dede was asked to come up on stage, and the paragraph honoring her was read out loud. When Dede spoke, she took something out of her pocket. I was shocked! Dede talked about how much she loved teaching and cared about the students and the school. Then she held up the little train engine. Dede said, "On the first day of school many, many years ago, Mr. Smith gave me a note and this little train. The note said 'The Edenvale train has left the station. Are you on board or not?' I have kept it all these years." Dede turned toward me and said, "Yes, Mr. Smith, I am still on board!"

Life Lesson: One never knows when a small thing will make a big and lasting impact.

My Wife Cost Me $50,000

In the 1990s, I started doing workshops on Integrated Thematic Instruction. Integrated Thematic Instruction (ITI) may still not be a common term; however, the concept is simple. Students learn more when what is being taught makes sense to them and when they can connect new ideas to something they already know. ITI is Velcro for a learner's mind. A good example of building on what a student already knows is mathematics. Each concept builds on a previously learned concept.

Integrated Thematic Instruction goes beyond a single subject area; it crosses subject areas. In sixth grade, the study of civilizations is the focus of history or social studies. ITI takes a look at what happens in a civilization across the curriculum.

Let's use the sixth-grade social studies unit on Ancient Egypt as an example.

- Students study the history of Ancient Egypt—pharaohs, pyramids, mummies, religious beliefs, and social customs.
- What could happen if we taught the unit on geometry at the same time?
- What could happen if we taught a science unit on geography or astrometry at the same time?
- What could happen if we integrated art at the same time?

- What could happen if we introduced the greatest library of the ancient world at the same time?
- What could happen if we used the unit as a basis for teaching nonfiction writing?

Most curricular areas (language arts, science, math, etc.) are taught in isolation and are self-contained. Integrated Thematic Instruction looks at how to make logical connections across the curricular areas. When subject areas are linked together in a natural way, students have lots of Velcro on which they can connect new learning. Velcro can help students make more sense about why they are learning something. Velcro can be a way to help students to see how things are interconnected.

Example: What would be more natural than linking the study of the pyramids, an important part of Egyptian cultural and religious life, with geometry? Think about area, volume, angles, measurement, and they are a natural fit with pyramids. Politics, history, science, music, art, literature are all happening at the same time. Each area affects other areas.

Teaching teachers how to look at teaching in this way isn't hard. No matter what subject is taught, it does not exist in a vacuum.

The idea was new to many teachers in 1991, but it is not hard. Teaching thematically does require thought, planning, and then practice, lots of practice. The payoff for students is being able to remember more content. The payoff is learning how to make connections and see what is happening around them more holistically. The payoff is discovering new things that may really excite them. Over time, students learn to see learning in a much broader context. Seeing things in broader contexts serves them well as adult citizens.

For several years, I trained teachers in Integrated Thematic Instruction through a five-week summer institute. For a week, a group of twenty teachers learned the fundamentals of the ITI approach to teaching. Teachers developed an integrated thematic unit for their particular grade level. After developing the unit, each teacher used it with students in summer school for four hours a day for four weeks...twenty days.

After students left for the day, the teachers continued with the ITI summer institute. The first part of each afternoon session was sharing and debriefing. What part of their thematic plan worked well and what did not go so well? The debriefing helped teachers see how their planning and teaching linked together in real time. The discussion was insightful and enriching; sometimes quite humorous. The second part of the afternoon was spent in modifying their ITI plan as well as preparing materials for the next day. By the end of the summer institute, teachers went away with a field-tested unit, new skills, and a way of thinking about instruction.

So how did my wife cost me $50,000? For several years, the Integrated Thematic Instruction summer institute was funded by a very large corporate foundation. One year, Barbara and I went out for dinner with the director in charge of educational projects and her husband. The four of us had a lot in common and enjoyed each other's company.

Just as I was ready to pitch the plans for the next summer institute, the foundation director turned to Barbara and asked about what was happening at her school. Barbara's school, Randol Elementary School, had a science emphasis. The foundation was sponsoring a program called the Mid-California Science Improvement Project (MCSIP). The director was looking for another school site in which to implement MCSIP. In short, Barbara walked away from dinner with *my* $50,000. To add insult to injury, Barbara's school continued to be funded for a total of five years…$250,000!

Life Lesson: "The best laid plans of mice and men often go astray."

A Carwash Changed the Future

Creating a positive environment...

Edenvale Elementary School was located in a very "at risk" neighborhood. However, was that a reason for a lack of student achievement or aspirations? Sure, the neighborhood dropout rate was 43 percent. Sure, most parents worked two or three jobs to put food on the table and pay the rent. Sure, the gang lifestyle was very attractive to teens that did not see much of a future. Sure, drugs were easily available. Those facts had nothing to do with how bright some of the kids growing up in the neighborhood were. To me, the "facts" were just excuses for poor academic achievement and not being able to do anything about the number of kids dropping out of high school. Simply not acceptable!

It did not take more than a couple of weeks to realize youngsters attending Edenvale were just as bright as the students attending schools "on the other side of the tracks." What most youngsters attending Edenvale were lacking were opportunities and resources.

The previous principal had done a fantastic job in turning the school around—cleaning out poor teachers and rebuilding the staff. My assignment was to develop a strong instructional program and increase student achievement.

The challenge was coming up with a way to help both students and parents see that other outcomes, instead of dropping out, could be viable. One fall afternoon, I was sitting at the Robertsville Car Wash waiting for my car to be finished. I noticed a very smartly dressed woman and her two sons walking over to their car. One boy was high school age and was wearing a jacket from Notre Dame University. The other boy was junior high school age and wearing a Georgetown University jacket. As they got into their brand-new "mile-long" Mercedes Benz, I thought about the environment in which the boys were growing up. These boys already knew they were going to college...they probably knew it before they were born. They had an abundance of opportunities and all the resources they could need available to them. Edenvale kids did not.

Those jackets, Notre Dame University and Georgetown University, stuck in my mind. The jackets were tangible symbols that reminded the boys every day that they were headed to college. Those jackets...tangible reminder? Could these two things become a way of changing the aspirations of Edenvale students?

What if Edenvale students had college T-shirts to wear? Could seeing themselves and each other in college T-shirts help change how they saw the future? I wondered.

Certainly, there were no funds to buy 640 college T-shirts for this crazy idea. However, could we find a way to get T-shirts donated? What if instead of asking colleges to donate shirts, we asked if we could adopt their college and ask for just one shirt?

In the next two months, with the help of Rosanne McGrath, an Edenvale student, and Rachel and Leah Smith, my two daughters, we sent letters to three hundred colleges and universities. The letter told a little about Edenvale School and asked if *we could adopt them.* Did they have a person with whom a student could be a pen pal? Lastly, we asked for a college shirt the pen pal could wear during assemblies as an ambassador for their college.

Within a few weeks, we had enough T-shirts to start an experimental program with the two sixth-grade classes...thus the Adopt-A-College program started.

In 1988, the Adopt-A-College program had two goals:

- Reduce the number of students who might drop out of high school.
  - There was research that third grader teachers could predict with 80 percent accuracy which students would be likely high school dropouts.

- Raise aspirations of students.
  - There was also research about interventions to change aspirations. If an intervention is introduced in junior high, the success rate is about 17 percent. If the same intervention is introduced before third grade, the success rate is about 80 percent.

The research was clear—the earlier the interventions, the higher the rate of success.

The following year, the Adopt-A-College program was expanded to other grade levels. By the third year, all classes, kindergarten through sixth grade, were participating in the program. After thirty-two years, the results speak for themselves, 866 former Edenvale students have been awarded scholarships totaling $632,750.

Life Lesson: Keep my eyes open. I never know when an idea or opportunity will present itself.

A Letter from a College Professor

Creating a positive future...

Somehow, a few weeks after starting the Adopt-A-College program, the media found out. An article appeared in the San Jose Mercury, and a story about this innovative program was featured on the local television station. Both stories did a nice job explaining the program and why it was created. I guess Adopt-A-College was one of those feel-good human interest stories that gets told by the media every once in a while.

The students were excited to read about their school in a newspaper article and see the story on television. Individual students were thrilled to see their own faces. Copies of the newspaper article were made and put up on bulletin boards in every classroom. The television news story was replayed on school television sets.

Parents and community members were very pleased with the positive press about Edenvale. It was the first positive stories about the Edenvale neighborhood in a long time.

The positive press also appeared to validate what we were doing. Students became more and more enthusiastic about writing the pen pals and receiving letters back. The media coverage gave a real boost to a fledgling program.

About a week after the newspaper article and the television story, I received a letter from a college professor. A college professor writing to us was a surprise. Eagerly, I opened the letter, and my heart fell through the floor.

In the letter, the professor condemned the Adopt-A-College program. In essence, he said that:

- the youngsters attending Edenvale were too brown, too black, and too poor;
- the youngsters attending Edenvale were too dumb to ever amount to anything;
- I should be ashamed of myself for starting such a program and giving poor children "false hope."

I could not believe it. I just sat at my desk, not believing what my eyes were reading. Why would anyone take the time to write such a letter, especially a college professor? The letter was hurtful, hateful, and racist. I did not share the letter with anyone for a very long time. I was shocked and I was very, very angry!

My anger toward this college professor changed about a year later. I suddenly realized what a favor the college professor's letter was, how I could use it to help the Adopt-A-College program. The letter ended up giving me tremendous resolve to absolutely prove him wrong. In the past thirty years, I have told the story of this letter many times to parents, educators, students, and funders.

I have been especially delighted in telling the story year after year to former Edenvale students who are graduating from high school and receiving a college scholarship from the Adopt-A-College scholarship program.

As of 2019, the Adopt-A-College scholarship program has awarded 866 scholarships, totaling about $632,500. Eighty-eight percent of the scholarships are actually used to continue an education in trade schools, community colleges, and universities. Eighty-two percent of the students complete a course of study and graduate. It is still hard for me to believe, but five Edenvalers have graduated from Stanford University and several having earned a PhD.

After sharing the letter each year, I thank the seniors receiving scholarships for proving the professor wrong for one more year! Edenvalers have now been proving the professor wrong for over thirty years!

Life Lesson: Sometimes inspiration and resolve come from very strange places. Don't miss it when it happens.

Out of *My* Mouth?

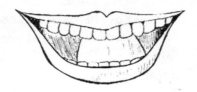

Creating a positive future...

The first year of the Adopt-A-College program was an experiment that included only sixth-grade students. The students, teachers, and I had a serious talk before starting the program. We all had questions.

- How would the Adopt-A-College program work in reality?
- Would pen pals actually write back to Edenvale students?
- What would be done with pen pal letters that were received?
- What would happen if one or two sixth graders did not receive a letter?
- Would the time and effort to write letters to pen pals really be worth the effort?
- What would be done with the college shirts that we received?

Together we came up with some answers. We all agreed that we were a part of an experiment, something that had never been tried before. The sixth graders were excited about creating something that had never been attempted.

Throughout the first year, we were surprised many times. The teachers and the students worked out problems that occurred.

- When a pen pal letter was received, the student receiving the letter would read it to the entire class so that everyone could learn new things about college.
- The original letter belonged to the student. Some students pinned their letters to the wall above their beds, and some others taped them to the mirror in the bathroom.
- The T-shirt donated by the college remained the property of Edenvale, to be washed and used year after year. Most shirts were worn for many years and finally replaced. Some of the college shirts were actually used for over twenty-five years.

The last day of school, we had a traditional awards assembly to acknowledge the efforts and accomplishments made by students throughout the year. After the assembly, I asked the sixth-grade teachers if their students could stay for a few minutes. I told the sixth-grade teachers they could leave and I would talk with the students alone.

I thanked the sixth graders for being willing to be part of the Adopt-A-College experiment. Over the summer, I had to decide whether or not to continue the program for the next school year. I said that I could not make the decision alone. I needed their honest feedback. Thinking about their experiences, what went well? What went wrong? What should be improved or changed? Should we actually continue the program?

Although I guided the discussion, we all sat on the cafeteria floor together as equals. I was surprised at how many students wanted to share. I was also surprised at the depth of the answers to some of the question I asked. What I thought might be a fifteen- or twenty-minute discussion lasted forty minutes. These sixth-grade students took the discussion seriously, and they also knew that I was taking them seriously.

"I appreciate your honesty about the Adopt-A-College experiment. You have created something that has never been tried before.

You can be proud of what you have done... Not many people your age ever have the opportunity to be part of an experiment. When you go to junior high next fall, there will not be an Adopt-A-College program. When you go on to high school, there will not be an Adopt-A-College program. Will the Adopt-A-College program really make a difference?"

At the end of the discussion, just before I sent them back to class, I said something that I had no idea I was going to say. (Husbands know the feeling well. Something slips out of our mouths, and there is no way the words can be shoved back in. However, our wives remember it forever). Well, something unintended slipped out of my mouth. "If you do your personal best in school and if you do not drop out, I will make you a promise. When you graduate from high school and choose to attend a trade school, community college, or university, I will give you a college scholarship to get started."

From where did that statement come? I had never even thought about scholarships. I had no money or any idea how to raise money for scholarships. There was no way I could shove the words back into my mouth, and a promise is a promise!

Fortunately, there were six years before these youngsters would graduate from high school. Since the dropout rate was so high and so few students continued any kind of education after graduation, I figured out that I could raise enough money to cover a few scholarships.

The sixth graders remembered my promise and they remembered it very, very well. Just before they graduated from high school, I received not five or six applications but twenty-seven. Instead of 43 percent dropping out of high school, the rate had fallen to 20 percent. Sometimes a problem can be a very good kind of problem. Fortunately, many friends, who believed in what we were doing, donated money, and we had enough to pay for twenty-seven scholarships to these pioneering students.

Life Lesson: Sometimes the things turn out far better than expected.

A Quarter Million What?

The following is one of my favorite anecdotes. After all these years, I cannot remember some of the exact details, but what happened is absolutely true.

Creating a positive future...

My assignment at Edenvale Elementary School was clear: develop a solid and cohesive K-6 instructional program, solidify parent support, and increase student achievement. By the time I arrived at Edenvale in 1988, the school had been turned around. "Reluctant dragons" on the staff had been replaced. The building had been purged of car seats and a lot of clutter. The new staff was pulling the instructional program together. There was a lot to be done to have a cohesive K-6 instruction program, but the base had been established by the time of my arrival.

As has been mentioned in other anecdotes, a large high school dropout rate, widespread poverty, drugs, and a school that "didn't work" for kids reinforced that Edenvale was a high-risk area in San Jose.

Developing a solid and cohesive K-6 program was not enough. Helping teachers change the way they planned and taught was not enough. Making moms and dads feel important and welcomed at Edenvale was not enough. Painting over tags on Saturday mornings was not enough. Working with gang members to help make Edenvale a neutral zone and a safe place for all little brothers and sisters, nieces and nephews was not enough.

The biggest challenge was to create and develop student buy-in. After an era in which students went to school because they had to and in which they were passive learners, a new norm had to be created. Teachers were doing many different positive things to engage the students in their classes. The challenge was creating school-wide buy-in, an environment in which children felt they *belonged*, in which children were coming to *their* school (ownership). The challenge was creating memorable experiences at school that would last children a lifetime. The challenge was creating a school where children knew they were getting a good education and had a future.

- "Student of the Week" and "Student of the Month" bumper stickers
- Green tickets
- Adopt-A-College program
- Wearing college shirts
- Monthly assemblies
- Guests from various colleges
- Crazy Dress-up days

Everything on the list helped create a positive school-wide environment.

One thing seemed to be missing: creating a school-wide environment where learning was fun as well as challenging. Since children becoming proficient readers are a major focus of elementary education, could anything be done to jumpstart student enjoyment of and achievement in reading?

After giving our "Student of the Week" and "Student of the Month" bumper stickers and listening to a guest speaker from a college, I challenged the student body.

"As you know, I know many people in San Jose and many people know about Edenvale School. The other day I had dinner with a friend. As usual, I was bragging about Edenvale. I told them about the teachers and about how clean the school is. Most of all, I was bragging about you…the students.

"My friend challenged me, 'What about reading? Edenvale students do not score very high on the state tests. They do not read enough books at school or at home.' Although I protested, my friend was right. Then he said 'Edenvale students are just not smart enough to ever become good readers.'"

That is the story I told at the assembly. There were puzzled looks on student faces and total silence. "I think my friend is wrong. I think Edenvale students are smart and can become better readers. Raise your hands if you think my friend is correct and that Edenvale students can never become good readers." A few hands were raised.

"Do you think that I am correct...that Edenvale students are smart and can read? How many of you would like to prove my friend wrong, *dead wrong*?" Almost every hand shot up!

Here is the challenge:

- Read library books (textbooks don't count).
- Read 250,000 pages in one month, about 10,000 pages per class.
- Every student has to participate if we are going to win.
- Every day, you must log the number of pages you read.
- Every day a parent or a teacher must sign that you read the number of pages.

"This is a huge challenge. The 250,000 pages are a lot to read, especially in just one month. Raise your hands if you think you can really do this." Again, hands shot into the air.

"OK, I will phone my friend and tell him the challenge is on! One last thing, if you win this challenge and prove my friend wrong, I make you a promise. I will sit on the school roof for an entire school day." The cheers were deafening.

Overnight, student log sheets appeared in every classroom. Teachers and students reviewed how to add to their personal log sheet each day. Teachers talked about the importance that a parent or teacher had to sign their log sheet...unverified pages do not count toward the 250,000 pages. (By the way, parents or older siblings could read books to kindergarten and first graders, and those pages counted.)

The race was on...250,000 pages in one month. Students that had never checked out a library book were now checking out books and devouring them. Students were reading in class, at recess, at home…anywhere they could. The challenge was off to a great start.

Somehow there always seems to be unintended consequences. Teachers saw some children were reading library books during math, language arts, and science lessons. We needed a quick fix. I made a school-wide announcement that reading library books while a teacher was teaching did not count. The challenge: how could we enforce the new rule?

Students were used to seeing me walk into their classroom and watch a lesson for a few minutes. What happened next, students did not expect. I saw a student reading a library book during a math lesson. Without a word, I walked over, took the book out of the student's hands, walked away, and left the classroom with book in hand. The look on the student's face was total disbelief! What was the student going to do? How was he going to get the library book back?

I started doing a lot of two to three minute visits to classrooms. I collected books from students who were reading instead of paying attention. If it was math or science time and I saw a library book even sitting on top of a student's desk, I picked it up too. Sometimes I would walk out with six or eight books. Sometimes I would sneak into a classroom when the students were at recess or lunch to "steal" books.

"How could Mr. Smith do this?" "Mr. Smith is stealing our books." "Does he want us to lose the bet?" "How do we get our books back?" The students were incredulous!

A strange thing happened. Students and teachers in each class began to form a library book "conspiracy." First, students became very careful about reading library books when they should be listening to a lesson. Second, some of the students would hide their library book underneath a textbook so I would not see it. Third, teachers would "steal" the library books back from me. As a result, student motivation to read was even higher, and students delighted when their teacher managed to "steal their books back from Mr. Smith's office."

Many teachers and students kept track of the total pages their class had read. Some classes posted the number of pages read on the bulletin board and changed the number daily. About the middle of the third week, students were getting a little smug and started slacking off. Time to up the ante!

I had become acquainted with the San Jose police officer, who had the day beat in the Edenvale neighborhood. Officer Ron was a fantastic police officer and very nice man. He was interested in the changes taking place at Edenvale School. Every couple of weeks, Officer Ron Daily would stop by just to check in.

Just when the number of pages being read started slowing down, Officer Ron happened to stop by. I told him I was concerned about the drop in the number of pages being read each day. I said to Officer Ron that I needed to up the ante to keep students engaged in winning the challenge. Together we hatched a plan.

When Officer Ron finished his shift, he came back to Edenvale with two large rolls of yellow "crime scene" tape. For the next hour, we took colored butcher paper and wrapped and taped every bookcase in the library. Then we sealed each bookcase with the yellow crime scene tape.

Yep, the library was closed. No books could be checked out. Bookcases had been covered with butcher paper and crime scene tape. The library had been declared a crime scene. You can only imagine the response by students. What were they going to do? How could they get more library books to read and win the challenge?

I was amazed (ha)! Students found ways to get to the nearby public library. They got library books and kept reading. After a few days, I began to see little mouseholes in the butcher paper. Students were secretly removing the crime scene tape, uncovering the book case, and finding the books they wanted to read. Students were also pretty good about resealing bookcases and reattaching crime scene tape.

After four weeks, it was time to add the total number of pages read in each classroom. A PA announcement was made for all teachers to send one student to the office with their classroom total. I took my time to add up all the pages. Tension grew throughout the school as students tried their best to pay attention to lessons.

Finally, we made the announcement. The students won the challenge. They had read almost 300,000 pages, well above the 250,000 required. Even in the office, I could hear cheers echoing through the building. Now it was my turn to pay up. We set a date for me to sit on the roof for an entire day.

The day came. The weather was perfect. The student body assembled on the lawn to see me climb the ladder to the roof. I wore a pink tutu. I also carried a fishing pole and a small pail with me. The students cheered as the ladder was removed so I could not secretly climb down.

Students checked up on me at recess time. They waved and had huge grins on their faces.

Lunchtime was a blast! The cafeteria planned a picnic lunch of hot dogs and hamburgers so the students could sit on the lawn below where I was sitting on the roof. Students called for me to use the fishing pole and lower the bucket. They stuffed the bucket several times with printed messages. I even tried to dance wearing my pink tutu. Students giggled and laughed and pointed at me. Paying off my part of the contest was great fun…I am not sure who had more fun—the students or me.

All these years later, former Edenvale students still remind me how they won and I had to sit on the roof.

> *Life Lesson: It takes a little planning and some work, but it is so worthwhile to create positive lifelong memories for youngsters.*

Edenvale Memories

(Paula Froeberg Ford)

Another point of view...

I have been teaching for over twenty years now. Whenever I hear or see the name Edenvale on Facebook or in the news, I can't help but succumb to the joyful memories that warm me up from the inside and put a smile on my face. I was lucky enough to be hired straight out of college by Meril Smith to teach a bilingual first-grade class. I fell in love not only with the children but the staff, community, and the heart of Edenvale. Though we were a low-income school in a struggling area of San Jose, California, the staff and community believed in what we were doing, and together we were accomplishing amazing things.

One day, Mr. Smith challenged our school to a Read-a-Thon. If the students in each class would read 10,000 pages, he would sit on the roof for an entire day. This was a huge task. Reading was not a daily habit for our community. Reading was a part of our curriculum, but students were not choosing to read for fun. Books were

141

not discussed or shared outside of class. Times were tough; families were concerned with paying the necessary bills, getting food on the table, and keeping a roof overhead. When dealing with daily struggles of food and shelter, it is tough to make reading be a top priority. However, the challenge was issued, and the students accepted the bet.

I filled my classroom with as many books as I could. Students began reading before school, at recess, lunch, and after school. We went to our school library each week, and students were eagerly checking out books and tracking their pages read. They were talking about books with their friends and sharing them back and forth.

Mr. Smith, not one to lose a bet easily, decided to play hardball. The first thing he did was close the school library. Imagine our surprise to find we could not go to the library to check out new books! Luckily, our upper-grade students were not to be denied. They researched the educational code and found out that it was illegal to close the school library. Undeterred, Mr. Smith tried new tactics.

Next, he came into our classrooms during recess and stole all our books. The children were incensed and motivated! Thanks to a helpful office secretary, we recovered our books and began locking our doors and windows! My first graders were convinced Mr. Smith would enter through the windows if they were left unlocked. Finally, every day during reading time, there would be a fire drill. Students remained steadfast and they took their books out to the fire drill exit locations and continued reading.

The students continued reading at home. They read to their parents and siblings and encouraged family members to read with them. Though this bet started with a challenge from Mr. Smith to the students of Edenvale, it became a domino effect to the entire community. Everyone was starting to read more often.

At the end of the Read-a-Thon, the students of Edenvale Elementary won the bet. Mr. Smith had to sit on the roof for a full school day. The local newspaper interviewed him and ran the story in the paper. The entire community celebrated the win. New reading habits were created not only with the students but also with the staff and community.

Mr. Smith sitting on the roof for an entire day was not so much a punishment, but rather a reward for instilling a love of reading in the students at Edenvale. I think he spent the day on the roof with his nose in a good book.

Be the Best We Can Be

(Linda Ullah)

My earliest memory of meeting Meril Smith was when I wanted to find a new school for my Special Day Class learners. I was not happy that my class was separate from the rest of the school. We were not an integrated part of that school. My fifth- and sixth-grade learners felt excluded. During a WASC evaluation of the school, one of my learners scratched out the words "Special Education" from my name tag. That was a huge eye-opener for me.

When it was suggested that Edenvale might take my class, I met with Meril. He agreed that we'd call my class a 5–6 combo class (within the school) and my learners would be fully integrated into every aspect of the school. I was thrilled. My learners went out to other classes as appropriate, headed up clubs, and participated in all school activities. After I moved to GATE and Title 1 teaching, Meril suggested that I include (informally) some of the Special Day Class learners in the GATE program. I loved working in a school where children were just children and not labels. Meril championed even my most challenging learners.

WE ARE ALL

WONDERFULLY MADE

After I'd transitioned into teaching the GATE (gifted and talented) Title 1 programs, Meril came to me and suggested that I have my learners do some research about the history of the school for the upcoming twenty-fifth anniversary of the school. I opened my big mouth to a newspaper reporter who happened to be at the school and said we were going to create a book, HyperCard stacks, etc. about the history of the school. I really had no idea how I was going to do this, but I'd seen projects other schools had done and I felt we could do this.

With Meril's support, I wrote to Apple Grant and got six networked computers, software, and a modem. We were on our way. The learners taught themselves how to create HyperCard stacks and later to use HyperStudio. It took students three years, but they published a book, *Edenvale 95111*, about the history of the Edenvale area.

Students also wrote a play about the history of the area and the school, which was performed by the drama club, and these young students created a local history museum at the school.

When the sixth-grade teachers wanted to have an awesome culminating social studies event, Meril supported them in creating an archeological dig on the school grounds. I have many memories of this dig, but the one that stand out are going shopping for artifacts with Meril. I remember going to a store that sold copies of Ancient Greek and Roman statues, pottery, etc. He talked them into giving us the broken ones for our dig. One night, Meril brought in a backhoe and buried these items along with bones. I worried that he'd get picked up by the police if they found him burying bones in the schoolyard, that he'd be arrested. In my imagination, I could see the headlines: "Edenvale Principal Arrested for Burying Bones." Fortunately, that never happened.

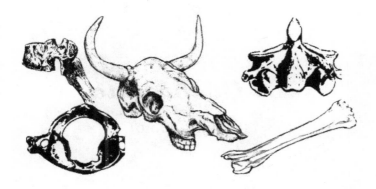

There are many more stories; however, the thing that was most special about Edenvale was its culture that encouraged all of us to be the best that we can be.

La Quebradita

(Carole Caputo)

It was April 1993. My young colleague, Jolene Franco, and I had decided to embark on our very first Cinco de Mayo production. Jolene chose to focus on the Battle of Puebla with her fourth graders, enlightening us all about why we were making such a big deal about this day. On the other hand, this particular fifth-grade teacher had discovered an incredibly talented group of fifth and sixth graders who had expressed some interest in performing a dance at the assembly. Game on!

My instructional assistant, Amelia, was persuaded to help with the choreography and to supervise rehearsals. I would periodically stop by the after-school practices to monitor progress and was quite impressed with the routine. One day, as I watched Luis and his cousin, Yesenia, dominating on the dance floor, I realized that one of the moves might not be totally acceptable for a school assembly.

After voicing my concerns, the kids convinced me that it was necessary for balance in the execution of the dance. I invited Mr.

Smith in to observe one of the rehearsals and held my breath while waiting for his reaction. He watched in silence and then, with a big grin across his face, proclaimed, "Wow! They are good!" After advising them to "low key" it on the thigh-to-thigh balance move, he enthusiastically gave them the go-ahead to proceed.

On the morning of the assembly, my chin hit the floor as a dozen or so very proud Latino students strutted onto campus. The boys sported cowboy hats, boots, and belts from which hung ribbons representing Michoacán, Jalisco, and Durango states where their families had once lived. The girls were not to be outdone. With heads held high, they were decked out in high boots, vests, and short shorts. Makeup was impeccably applied and hair perfectly coiffed.

Too late! Our fabulous dancing group looked amazing...but ready for dancing at a nightclub. The show must go on! I prayed I would still have a job.

On the stage, the younger students had performed their sweet routines, Jolene's battle had been fought, and it was time for the grand finale, "La Quebradita." As the performers sashayed into their places, whispers permeated the room. The music started, and the dancers confidently broke out into their number. Seeing that the routine was not like the standard Cinco de Mayo choreography they were accustomed to, the audience was abuzz.

Sensing that the dancers might need a bit of audience participation, Mr. Smith immediately began clapping enthusiastically to the music. It didn't take long for the crowd to join in. The entire auditorium was rockin',' and the dancers had everyone mesmerized. Parents, staff, and students loved it. The finale was truly grand!

Needless to say, I doubt that a great deal of learning took place for the remainder of the day for these kids. I do know, however, that they were on cloud nine and were thoroughly enjoying their "celebrity" status. After the assembly, that talented group of students was eventually asked to perform at three additional events in the area. Word was out that these kids could dance!

Many years later, on a beautiful afternoon in May, I heard a gentle knock on my classroom door. There stood Luis with a couple of his high school buddies. A big grin flashed across his face as he asked, "Can we watch the video?" No further explanation was needed. I quickly found that dusty old VHS tape of Edenvale's '93 Cinco de Mayo Assembly and fast-forwarded to "La Quebradita." As I watched his beaming face and listened to the excitement in his voice, I knew that our goal of creating memories for our students had been accomplished. I hope Luis and Yesenia are still dancing!

Bones!

(Ginny Maiwald, Past Edenvale Principal)

The late 1990s brought much-needed structural changes to the Edenvale building. Demolition, trenching, construction, and relocation of portable classrooms were daily occurrences. Edenvale School underwent a much-needed modernization project, ushering the school into the new century. I was the principal at the time, and it had been six or seven years since Meril had left. One day, something happened that caused me to make an unanticipated phone call.

GINNY: Hi, Meril. Before we begin, I want you to know that I'm in the Edenvale School principal's office with local authorities who are listening to this conversation. I need to put you on speaker, as we have some questions for you.

MERIL: Oh, how may I help?

GINNY: We have an unusual situation and we need to ask you some questions.

MERIL: Sure, what's your question?

GINNY: Are you aware that bones are buried at the back of the school site?
MERIL: (pause and then hysterical laughter> Yeah, that was me!

Inside the building walls, transition was also happening at Edenvale School. The student population had become so large that families were offered places at the newest school. The district offered incentives for them to leave Edenvale and attend the new school.

Families simply did not want to move their children from Edenvale School. Student achievement soared as the academic indicators were showing that Edenvale was a top performing school in comparison to similar schools in the state. Teachers were working hard before, during and after school; and Edenvale students knew that college was to be a part of their future.

At the same time, the staff was also facing events that brought the issues associated with a campus under construction and the daily challenges of school life into perspective. Beloved longtime fifth-grade teacher, Margaret Ivey, had been diagnosed with terminal cancer. This vibrant redhead energized the staff, held high expectations for her students, and held a special place deep in the soul of Edenvale School. It was with heavy hearts that we had to say goodbye to Margaret Ivey.

The staff threw a baby shower for a new teacher; certainly a new baby and a party would lift spirits! Shortly after, we learned the baby girl was stillborn. Still more tragedy struck when a student witnessed the murder of his mother on Christmas Day.

Through these challenges, the Edenvale way reminded staff and students of how we belonged to one another. Students felt the increased doses of attention and genuine caring and support. They flourished and continued to *soar* in their academic and social skills.

It was during this time that bones were discovered at the back of the campus. There were dozens of bones, including skulls, buried not far from the surface. Other items were discovered—bits of pottery, plates, and glassware. Not wanting to alert staff until accurate information was available and anticipating the worst, I contacted local authorities. While authorities examined the area, veteran teacher Carole Caputo, always a late worker, came out of her classroom and asked what was going on. Carole's reaction was surprising. With a grin, she said, "Contact Meril Smith right away."

Edenvale School holds a long-standing reputation of bringing basic skills to life in every way possible. Thematic instruction, singing, dance, Adopt-A-College assemblies, a community-wide pancake breakfast, magic shows, scholarship nights, classes for parents, the Boys and Girls Club, and a small community center all make this school and learning the heart of the community. The neighborhood has an association, the Edenvale Roundtable, and everyone took pride in this vibrant school. Another former principal, Robert Topf, also a musician, wrote songs and scripted shows the students and staff performed and sang.

In this unique Edenvale traditional fashion, history was also brought to life. Greek mythology wasn't simply studied; the campus was transformed into a Grecian temple, and students dressed up and role-played. Learning about archaeology through reading history books just wouldn't do for Edenvale students; an archeological dig was planned, prepared, and constructed.

My phone call to Meril took me back. I was not prepared that each question brought a new wave of laughter. This had not been just an experience for the students. Staff came together in party mode for these occasions. Through the years, staff members had buried anything and everything. What more was to be found was anyone's guess!

The idea of an archaeological dig, like so many Edenvale traditions, took on a synergy with the staff. This resourceful staff did not purchase items; the archaeological dig would have the authentic look of history. The previous night's chicken bones and last Sunday's pork shoulder, broken plates, pottery and other household relics were determined to appropriately duplicate the true archaeological experience of excavation for students. Meril had even obtained a few skulls. No one exactly took note of where and what was collected and buried. Some years relics from previous years would appear, and some years areas were left untouched...until years later when modernization workers stumbled upon an area so unusual that the administration was called upon.

While it took me longer to find the humor in the situation, the authorities, longtime friends of Edenvale, knew our culture and how random bones found in this schoolyard were part of the unique learning process this school embodies.

Part 5

1980's

Growing Up
Edenvale

(1980–2000)

Growing Up Edenvale

(Jason Hansen)

Growing up as an Edenvale Eagle truly made an impact on the person I am today. Our neighborhood may have been run-down and filled with drug dealers and gangs, but Mr. Smith was responsible for bringing change to the community. My parents each served as PTA president at different times, and all three of my brothers attended Edenvale as well. It was clear that our family truly loved the school primarily because of its innovative and passionate principal, Mr. Meril Smith. He mentored a remarkable faculty, encouraged families to get involved, and developed thousands of lifelong learners.

Edenvale regularly organized fun and engaging events for students outside of the classroom, which to this day are some of my favorite memories from elementary school. One ongoing event was Olympic Day, where classes cycled through a variety of obstacle courses, races, and challenges spread out over the schoolyard.

For another event, Edenvale brought in emergency response personnel for a safety day. At their own stations, firemen, paramedics, and police officers spoke to classes about emergency services while allowing students to ask questions, try on equipment, and climb inside their emergency vehicles. To further develop a mindset of safety in his students, I vividly recall one year where Mr. Smith had the younger students out on the field watching the older students slowly come out of the school "wounded" (with bandages and fake blood) or "dead" to show the seriousness of being prepared for dangerous events like earthquakes and fires.

The teachers I had at Edenvale are the ones who inspired me from an early age to want to become a teacher. Mr. Smith had a huge part in empowering his teachers to find ways to make learning matter in the lives of their students. As a kindergartner, I can still recall learning the Pledge of Allegiance in ASL (American Sign Language) with Mrs. San Bui and making stone soup with Mrs. Hala Saah in first grade. I remember assembling piñatas in third grade with Mrs. Laura Vivit and protecting a raw egg for the yearly egg drop in fourth grade with Mr. Erik Sorensen.

In 1991, Mr. Smith worked hard to get computers donated for our upper-grade classrooms to become the "Classrooms of the Twenty-First Century." As a fifth grader with Mrs. Margaret Ivy, I can remember having a computer in between every two students to share. We frequently used them to type our essays on and do research, and at the time, we felt so special! Later as a sixth grader with Mrs. Angie Ortega, I can recall spending hours to construct our own Egyptian museum in the school library for the rest of the school to visit. Utilizing the hands-on lessons I participated in as a child at Edenvale has definitely shaped the way I approach my own teaching today.

One year, the local news team came and interviewed him up on the roof! Students could ask him questions throughout the day by putting messages in a bucket that he would pull up to the roof to read. Another year, he was forced to wear hot pink clothing and accessories brought by students while stuck on the roof. As a kid, it was awesome seeing your principal in a pink tutu!

Dating back to kindergarten, I can still remember the assemblies Edenvale would organize. Because I did not have any college graduates in my immediate family, Edenvale's Adopt-A-College assemblies were exciting. Listening to real-life college students speak to us while I was wearing a college sweatshirt solidified my desire to graduate from college. To this day, I remember how every assembly ended. Mr. Smith would lead the school in a chant, "No one can do everything, but everyone can do something, and when we work together, we accomplish amazing things!"

As a child, I never thought about how much time and effort it took for Mr. Smith to establish the Adopt-A-College program. He must have written to hundreds of colleges and universities to get pen pals for every student each year! Adopt-A-College was the initial spark to get students excited about going to college. I remember the excitement when one of my classmates would get a letter or care package from a pen pal. One year, I had a pen pal from Cal State Fullerton who sent my entire class pencils. We thought we had won the jackpot! I read my pen pal's letter to the class and imagined what college life would be like someday.

The most remarkable part of the Adopt-A-College program was that Mr. Smith promised every single student that if they graduated from high school, he would have some type of scholarship waiting for them to get started in college. Six years later, he fulfilled his promise and had a scholarship waiting for me to attend San Jose State University.

I'll never forget the love that Meril Smith had for me, my family, my peers, and my teachers. I pray I can be an educator like him for the children and families with whom I come in contact during my career.

Everyone Can Accomplish Something

(Maria Mejia)

When remembering my time at Edenvale Elementary School, I was overcome with many different memories and emotions. The one constant theme through all of it was dedication. As I found out later, the dedication of my principal, Meril Smith, not only made my experience unique but it also continued to impact my life. I would not be the person I am without him.

Mr. Smith taught us the value of unity and understanding the world around us. He drilled into our heads that "no one can accomplish everything but that everyone can accomplish something." Mr. Smith challenged us to always do our personal best, and I continue to give that same challenge to my children.

Sara Remembers

(Sara Hill)

All I really know is that college wasn't a question in my life. I was going to college; the question was always, where? I was first introduced to the idea of college at the age of ten. I enrolled in a new school, Edenvale Elementary, where I started fifth grade. I didn't know how much this new school would impact my life, but it did significantly!

At Edenvale, not only was I told I was going to college but I was also told I'd be given money to go to college. That was *big*! At the beginning of the year, there were all these college shirts hanging from the ceiling in Mr. Eric Sorensen's classroom. I remember being told to pick one to wear every month at our Adopt-A-College assemblies. I chose a pretty purple one and cringed at some of the shirts my classmates chose.

We spent class time writing to college pen pals and asking questions about college. Most college students would write back! Some would even send packages of stuff! When we got letters, fifth graders stood in front of the classroom and read their letters out loud. Sometimes they showed the class all the cool stuff they got from their pen pals. I always chose pretty shirts. I never got anything in the mail. I learned a lesson: appearances do not equate to a quality relationship! Even still, I looked forward to our assemblies and the opportunity to wear a pretty college shirt. At assemblies, we would listen to all the different keynote speakers that would come to tell us that going to college was attainable.

College would change our lives and reinforce Mr. Smith's saying that I still recite to this day, "No one can do everything, but everyone can do something, and when we work together, we accomplish amazing things!"

I Am an Edenvale Kid

(Ashley Wiggins, Class of 1998)

When I think of Edenvale, I remember all the awesome experiences in the GATE (Gifted and Talented Education) program with our teacher, Mrs. Linda Ullah. I looked forward to being pulled out of class in the afternoon to go to the computer lab and learn how to make movies on the Mac computers. I also *loved* the field trips to space camp at Moffett field, the Rosicrucian Egyptian Museum, and Monterey Bay Aquarium. Mrs. Ullah was an amazing teacher.

One of my fondest memories while attending school at Edenvale was participating in Olympic Day. This was a day where every classroom got to spend the entire day outside, on a beautiful spring day, and participate in a bunch of different games, activities, and competitions. We looked forward to that day every year and to eating barbecue hot dogs and cheeseburgers at our picnic lunch. Olympic Day represented the school year coming to an end and getting ready to enjoy the summer. I have always appreciated having Olympic Day.

The very first Halloween Carnival we had was in second or third grade. We helped set up the various gaming booths and decorations. I remember how great a turnout there was and feeling so happy and lucky to be able to have such an experience with my family and friends. When I reminisce about Edenvale, the Halloween Carnival always comes to mind.

Sadly, I remember when our office secretary, Julie Fox, announced that she was transferring to a brand-new school. Every class dedicated some classroom time to learn the song "Stand by Me." I remember the *whole* school sat outside on the grass and sang the song to her, showing our appreciation for her and how important she was to us. I remember her crying because of the gesture.

During the spring every year (I think when I was in fourth grade and up), staff from the local Boys and Girls Club (BGC) would come to campus during our lunch recess to ref flag football games, soccer games, and other fun games. I remember Adam and Fred and Mo (the BGC staff) would use these opportunities to recruit kids to join the Boys and Girls Club. I joined every year up until I was in high school. I loved my time there so much that I actually ended up becoming a staff member at the Menlo Park BGC a few years after I graduated college.

After working for the Boys and Girls Club for two years, I moved in 2011 to Denver Colorado to attend graduate school at the University of Denver. I graduated with a master's in clinical social work with and emphasis in child welfare and trauma. Although living and working in Denver as an adult, I am proud having grown up as an Edenvale kid.

Bilingual

(Anna Olagues, Class of 1994)

From the young age of six or seven, I had convinced myself that speaking Spanish was a negative thing. I was held back in first grade for not knowing enough English and always struggling with reading and spelling. As a young kid, I was embarrassed of my cultural background and did not like to speak in Spanish at school. Often when people spoke to me in Spanish, I would reply to them in English. That all changed when I was in fourth grade with Mr. Marich.

I still remember sitting on the carpeted floor of the classroom facing Mr. Marich as he sat in front of a green chalkboard. We had learned about college majors and were sharing our career aspirations with him so he could aid us in choosing a college major. When it was my time to share, I told the class I wanted to be a teacher. I already knew he would say "educator" because a previous student had also shared that she wanted to be a teacher. However, I did not expect what occurred next.

Mr. Marich suggested that I major in education, but rather that I major in bilingual education. Up until that moment, I had never heard of the word *bilingual,* so I raised my hand and asked what it meant. Mr. Marich lit up as he began to explain bilingualism. That was the first time I had ever heard a grown-up, a teacher, tell me that kids who spoke two languages were smart because they knew twice as much vocabulary. He also went on to tell us that knowing certain languages was helpful in understanding difficult words in English. I still remember that he used the word *cargo* as an example.

At some point in the conversation, another student raised his hand and asked if speaking Mexican was the only kind of bilingual. Mr. Marich explained that knowing any two languages meant that you were bilingual. He also clarified for the class that people do not speak Mexican and that Mexicans were not the only Spanish speakers. It was at that point that I raised my hand. "My mom is from El Salvador," I announced to the class. Mr. Marich again lit up with enthusiasm. He quickly pulled down a world map that was rolled up above the chalkboard and pointed out to us that many countries spoke Spanish, including El Salvador.

The next day, I arrived at school with a plate of pupusa and a small El Salvador flag for Mr. Marich. For the first time ever, I was proud of my heritage and proud to be a native Spanish speaker. Up until that point, I had seen being bilingual as a chore at school. I had to continuously translate for teachers and peers and did not like having to do so. However, after hearing Mr. Marich, I realized that my bilingualism was a talent. I was able to do something my teacher could not. I could understand and speak in Spanish.

It was after that day that I began to read and write in Spanish. Mr. Marich had seen something special in me. He inspired me to want to further develop my billiteracy. At the end of that school year, Mr. Marich presented me with a social studies award for "Bringing El Salvador to Life!" That was one of my favorite awards as a kid.

As I look back, I am thankful for that moment on the carpet. Realizing the value of bilingualism and having it validated by a teacher was something very powerful to me. In college, I majored in child development and participated in Aztec dancing and barrio art and traveled to several Latin American countries. After receiving my bilingual teaching degree from UC Davis, I taught dual immersion in Spanish and English for six years. Currently I am the ELD representative on my school's leadership team and hope to someday be a school principal for a Latino community.

Reflections

(Camille Littlejohn)

Reflecting on my time at Edenvale, I realize just how impactful it was in forging who I am today. My education, confidence, and determination all stem from my experience at Edenvale. Words cannot express the gratitude I have for Mr. Smith and his staff, but that will not stop me from trying.

I was lucky to have been raised to have a genuine love for education, and Edenvale gave me the road map to accomplish my goals. Early on, they taught me that going to college was for everyone, not just a select few. It did not matter how much money my family had or where we came from; we mattered and were valued.

The Adopt-A-College program was instrumental for making college seem real and accessible. The ability to converse about college life through mail with a college student as an elementary school student blew my mind and made college relatable and attainable. I came to understand that college could drastically improve and change the direction of my life for the better.

I look back on my time with Mr. Smith and teachers like Mrs. Ivy, Mrs. Fukasawa, and Mr. Bowlin as the foundation of my love for reading, giving, and higher learning. These wonderful people had a profound impact on my life by embodying the very ideals they taught. I recall a Read-a-Thon challenge where if the goal was met, Mr. Smith would spend an entire day on the roof! What kid wouldn't want to see that? Inspired at the prospect, the school blew past its reading goals, and Mr. Smith happily paid his debt. This unique act showed us the importance of reading and goal setting, but it also demonstrated the love and commitment Mr. Smith had for his students and the school.

In addition to education, Edenvale emphasized the importance of community and family. For example, we would adopt families for the holidays to give presents, clothes, and food. When I broke my arm and had to stay in the hospital, a group of classmates brought me gifts and cards to cheer me up. Even at eight years old, I understood the significance of the love I was receiving from my community and how much that meant to me.

I am extremely grateful for the support I received at Edenvale. I ran a hard and competitive race for student council in sixth grade and lost. The staff not only wiped my tears but also encouraged me to start my own club, which resulted in about twenty-five kids joining. Our hand-clapping club preformed multiple times in front of the school and at local events. Starting that club showed me from a young age that I could organize, hold a group's attention, and form skills I still use to this day. The experience helped me learn that life may not always go your way, but it's what you learn from it and what you do after that can help you excel.

I am so thankful for the time, energy, love, and hope that were given the students at Edenvale. My Edenvale experience gave me the strong foundation and confidence that I later leveraged to put myself through college and start my own business. I don't know if I would have been able to accomplish everything if Edenvale hadn't laid the groundwork for perseverance and a love of learning. I can definitively say that I'm a better person as a result of my years at Edenvale. These gifts that were given to me are priceless and have inspired me in my everyday life to pay it forward. In fact, I chose a parent participation school for my children and try to encourage the same love of education and perseverance to a new group of children. Thank you, Edenvale!

New Ways to Learn

(Sara Hill)

Even as a child, I realized that the way I was "allowed" to learn at Edenvale was different. Here are a few things that vividly stick out in my mind.

- *Oregon Trail*

Once a week, I was allowed to die of some miserable disease while playing Oregon Trail on the computer. And for whatever reason, I *knew* this was a privilege.

- *Egg Drop*

I remember being in the fifth grade and each student came up with our own theory and prototype for how to drop an egg from the school roof without it breaking. I remember using a Halloween bucket, padding, and tape. Yes, my egg broke. I don't remember which contraptions didn't break eggs, but I remember putting a lot of time and energy into that science project.

- *Cultural Awareness and Diversity*

Edenvale was a blend of students from all races and ethnicities. In the fifth grade, our class would do a cultural diversity and awareness parties where each student would bring in a dish from their culture and we had a big potluck... I loved that!

- *The Battle of Big Little Horn*

My teacher, Mr. Sorensen, was a bit of a hippy (this, of course, I realized in retrospect). When learning about the Battle of Big Little Horn, he brought in an old 45 record and record player...it didn't even have vinyl on both sides. He played the record, and we dissected the song, wrote all of the words to the song, and eventually sang the song together as a class. I still remember this song (decades later): "The Indians gather to have a war dance, out along all along Big Little Horn, each brave had a bow, a shield and a lance, and out on the prairie they started to dance. Black Low Dog, Spotted Eagle, Red Horn, and Dawn. Two Moons, Little Knife, and Sitting Bull, the chief of them all, yes Sitting Bull, the chief of them all!" I have tried to google the lyrics, but I have been unsuccessful in locating the name and artist responsible for the song.

• *Ancient Egypt*

   In the sixth grade, my teacher, Mrs. Ivey, was simply amazing. She and the other sixth-grade teachers got to together and created a whole board game themed on Ancient Egypt! At the end of the day, we'd get into groups that were assigned and work collaboratively with students from other classrooms. Each team had a version of the game, and we had to discover stuff about ancient Egypt and decode hieroglyphics. We had six weeks to accomplish this task. It was such an innovative and creative way to get us to study. Although Howard Gardner's Multiple Intelligences theory was fairly new at the time, this game engaged all of the intelligences to meet curricular outcomes! And at the end, we took a field trip to the Rosicrucian Egyptian Museum to witness firsthand the content we had been learning about for the previous six weeks.

   Edenvale had a strong emphasis on basic skills. However, we were expected to apply the basic skills in different and exciting ways.

Looking Back

(Joanne Song)

Looking back on my childhood, my educational experience is what I mostly think about. Edenvale was my home. I can't say I have a particular favorite memory, but I remember the feelings of always feeling safe and cared for.

As an adult, I better understand that that this actually should not have been the case. I remember learning that just before I moved into the neighborhood, Project Crackdown was there the year before; crack houses were cleaned up, the streets were not safe, and crime was prevalent. With the history of drug problems in the community, having the neighborhood police, firefighters, and EMTs come and talk about safety created awareness on what to avoid in life.

As I grew older, I remember being tempted by the gang culture. I fully understand that it could have been me, but I recognize that Edenvale was a large contributing factor in providing me a strong foundation to make sure gangs weren't going to be my future. The culture that Mr. Smith created in the school was a true gift. Working as an educator now, I know the importance of leadership creating culture in a school and how much it can trickle down to all the staff and then to the children.

Today I see that school events at Edenvale were intentionally designed for the needs of the community. Living in a diverse community, we celebrated each other during Cultural Days, and I didn't have to be ashamed for being a minority.

Knowing that literacy levels were low, Mr. Smith created a school-wide Read-A-Thon that really pumped up the whole school to read more (even if that meant he sat on the school's roof wearing a pink tutu).

Understanding most people from my community did not go on to higher education, the Adopt-A-College program was born. We got excited about college from a young age, and our excitement grew when we wrote to college students and visited local colleges. I personally went on to get my master's degree in communicative disorders and have worked with children with special needs in multiple types of communities.

Although Edenvale focused on a strong basic skills program, it also created a platform for well-roundedness. It encouraged environmentalism, the arts, and knowing how to be a good person. I think the staff understood that while school is ultimately responsible for our academic education, education goes beyond the books. Reflecting back on the strategic ways that Edenvale has shaped my life, I'm eternally grateful for the foundation it has created for who I am today.

I hope that I am giving back to others the same way that Mr. Smith and all my teachers gave so much to me.

A Mom Goes to College

(Rene McGrath)

There I sat in another stirring Adopt-A-College assembly at Edenvale Elementary School. I'm not sure if it was the visiting president of Smith College or a local representative for San Jose State University, but I looked around the cafeteria packed with kindergarten through sixth-grade students sitting so quietly in their own Adopt-A-College T-shirts and thought to myself, *What a great program this is...inspiring these little kids to set the goal of attending college!* As a mother of five children, I was so grateful that my kids were being exposed to the idea of attending college and that it could be a reality for them.

Not long after that assembly, I was sweeping the floor in my kitchen. I distinctly heard a voice in my head tell me that the dream of attending college was for me also. That happened in December of 1990, and by January, I had enrolled in our local Evergreen Valley Community College. Our youngest child was three years old, and she was eligible to attend the preschool on campus if I would volunteer. So there we were, going to college together!

I graduated with my AA in 1992 and then attended class at San Jose State University.

Due to the economy, our family had to sell our house, and we moved to Cedar City, Utah, where I earned a bachelor's degree in Education at Southern Utah University. Our family then relocated to Roseville, California, where I became an elementary school teacher. I went on to earn a master's degree in reading and a reading certificate that allowed me to teach hundreds of children the skill of reading. I have also earned an administration credential.

Now after over twenty years in education, I can't thank Mr. Meril Smith and his vision of the Adopt-A-College program for the difference it was made in my life and my family!

All of our five children have graduated from college—one has become a teacher, one has an MBA, two have associate's degrees, and one has a bachelor's degree. All of our sons and daughters-in-law have graduated from college, and three have master's degrees. I'm confident that this wouldn't have happened without the Adopt-A-College program! The oldest of my grandchildren are already attending college, so that makes three generations that have been influenced by this amazing program!

Leadership

(Sara Hill)

In sixth grade, I was elected student body president. Being student body president afforded me the opportunity to get to know Mr. Smith better than many students at Edenvale School. As the student body president, I was afforded great opportunities that have had a lasting impression on my life.

The first opportunity that changed my life was when I attended a leadership conference. I was one of very few elementary school students there. There were teachers, administrators, and high school students who were incredibly talented. I had an awesome time at that conference and I can say it was probably my first experience with formal leadership.

I remember during lunch sitting next to a teacher from my school and the teacher asked what school we were from. When we responded with "Edenvale," the other teacher put her lunch down and started to make bowing gestures. It shocked me to see a professional from another school respond so strongly toward my school and in a positive way. The teacher then shifted the credit to great leadership and specifically named Mr. Smith. I went home with a new perspective on how special my school was.

The second thing that happened was when I got to meet and introduce the Mayor of San Jose, Susan Hammer, at an Adopt-A-College assembly. It was a *big* deal. My dad came from work to watch me introduce the mayor. My brother and I took pictures with her afterward, and we were invited to do a private viewing/tour of her chambers. I don't remember much from the actual tour but I do remember feeling special.

Soon after that, Mr. Smith called my home and asked me if I would fly to Los Angeles with him and my father. I was asked to speak to the California Association of Financial Aid Administrators. We worked diligently on my speech. I practiced it. I had to learn "We Are the World" to sing with other young people who would be there. I practiced that too. I picked my favorite dress, fancied my hair, and my father and I were off to the airport.

I stood in front of the California Association of Financial Aid officers sprinkled with other important people whose titles I cannot remember. I spoke about the Adopt-A-College Program and the Read-A-Thon and how both of these programs had personally impacted my life at the young age of ten. I used big words and I delivered my speech well. Adults kept coming to me to tell me what a great job I did and how impressed they were. Politely I smiled and thanked them. Some folks engaged my dad too.

The thing I most enjoyed was the dinner and the dance party where I danced the evening away with my father. This event was actually my highlight as a child. As an adult, I see how those early experiences have manifested in my life.

Later that year, Mr. Smith tapped me again to participate in a PSA with Kenny Loggins where I was able to sing his song, "If you Believe," with him and a group of high school students. Initially I didn't know who he was, but it didn't matter. I was in a commercial! I ate lunch and broke bread with this man. I was singing his song alongside of him. Although I didn't fully understand the gravity of what I was doing at the time, these are cherished memories…all provided by my elementary school. These were moments that shaped my character, integrity, and view on leadership and education.

The final honor that I had did not occur while I was in school at Edenvale. As I began my senior year of high school, my phone rang and Mr. Smith was on the other line. I had completely forgotten the promise he made me—that if I was going to college, he'd give me a scholarship to get started. He reminded me of his promise and asked me to help find other Edenvale classmates who were also planning on going to college…any college, not just four-year institutions. And per usual, I put my full effort into doing a great job.

At Scholarship Night, we were awarded our scholarships. My class was the largest class of scholarship recipients, and even included a student who had relocated to Colorado. All this was before social media existed! That was a feat!

I was proud of these accomplishments, but more so, I was proud to stand on the same stage…the same stage that Mr. Smith challenged us from, the same stage where I'd met the Mayor of San

Jose and shook her hand. It was the same stage I had a part in *The Wizard of Oz* and the play *Edenvale 95111*. This was the same stage I used to introduce guest speakers and the same that I delivered my first speech.

Here I was again standing on the same stage that gave me all these awesome and amazing opportunities…as I stood there to receive *my* Adopt-A College scholarship that was promised to me so many years before.

My family gave me an amazing foundation at home. Edenvale and Mr. Smith provided the foundation to become a lifelong learner, not just a lifelong learner but one with an altruistic heart.

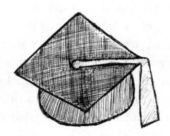

Mr. Smith's impact on my life has been profound, and I am so happy to still be in contact with him. Every time I receive another degree, Mr. Smith is invited to the ceremony.

More than Just a T-Shirt

(Daisy Vallesfino)

Sifting through a huge box of oversized college T-shirts, my choices seemed limitless—which one do I choose? There were so many. I proceeded to pick one and joined my classmates in line to go to the cafeteria for the assembly.

The Adopt-A-College program was by far one of the most memorable and impactful experiences I've had. I attended Edenvale Elementary School from 1996 to 2003, kindergarten to sixth grade, and it was during those crucial years that my life could have taken a different route than it did if not for the support provided by my teachers, principals, and the Adopt-A-College program.

On assembly days for the Adopt-A-College program, perhaps just as exciting as the assembly itself was the college T-shirt choice we made right before the assembly. During my years at Edenvale, we were able to choose from a large selection of shirts from vari-

183

ous colleges, and that in it of itself was beautiful—the *choice*. Each assembly I wore a different college's shirt. I wanted to test out all of them at some point. There was something magical about the options, and as I reflect on the experience, I now understand what that seemingly simple act of choosing a shirt symbolized—*possibility*. To anyone else, they might've just seen a young girl obsessing over color and design, but in reality, it was a young girl sifting through her possible future.

To give some perspective, my family background was definitely not the most ideal environment for supporting success. My parents emigrated from the Philippines, neither of them familiar with the US education system. In addition, my half brother, who also was born and raised in the Philippines, came to the US in his twenties and didn't pursue any further schooling when he got here. My half sister, who is eighteen years older than me, was already out of the house by the time I was born. Not helping the situation, she was a high school dropout. So educationally, my family was not the prime example for success. We didn't do any better financially. While my father tried his best when I was young, he suffered from a work injury around 2000 to 2001 that put him on permanent disability, ending his working career. Further stress was added in 2002 when my mother suffered from a major health issue that had her hospitalized and undergoing surgery, and we weren't sure how she would fare afterward. All of this took place while I was a student at Edenvale. It is safe to say that I could've ended up on a very different path if not for Edenvale and the Adopt-a-College program. From the staff to the assemblies to the pancake breakfasts that supported the program and students, Edenvale kept me looking forward.

Fast-forwarding to high school, I worked hard and took as many AP classes as I could. When senior year came, everything that Edenvale had conditioned me to strive for became a reality. During college application season, I had no idea what I wanted to major in or where I should go—the only thing I knew for sure was that *I was going*, wherever that might be. Then came the acceptances, of which I was accepted to every college to which I applied.

I couldn't help but recall the box of college T-shirts and making a choice of what to wear for the assembly, but this time it was real, and I chose UCLA. So spring of 2009, I sent in my college acceptance letter to Edenvale, attended the pancake breakfast, and received the scholarship that they had promised. That scholarship allowed me to purchase the laptop I ended up using my entire time at UCLA, and even a few years after, as well as the textbooks I needed for my first quarter of classes. In a way, Edenvale Elementary came with me to college.

The impact of Edenvale doesn't end there. Senior year came again, this time in college. I wasn't sure what I wanted to do, but that's the whole point—*I had options*, just as I had options with the box of T-shirts. That's what college gives you and that's what Edenvale taught me to strive for. So I spent the year reflecting on what was important to me, and the same thought always came to mind—education. So I made the decision to teach. I went to the UC Davis School of Education to get my credential and master's degree in education, and I am now a high school biology, chemistry, and AP Chemistry teacher.

All in all, the reach of Edenvale and its Adopt-A-College program is immeasurable. It sparks interest in college, or if the spark was there, it brings college into reach. It highlights the importance of learning because we're going to be doing that the rest of our lives. College, whichever one you go to, enhances the quality of that learning, but most importantly, it gives us opportunity. Yes, someone might want to go into a profession that doesn't necessarily require a four-year degree, but having that as *one* of many options instead of the *only* option is why I strongly believe in the message that Edenvale and the Adopt-A-College program instill, and I take that message every day to work with me when I get up in front of my students and teach.

And to think my journey began with just a box of oversized college T-shirts.

Boat People

(Nhu "Jenny" Le)

The term "boat people" became known to the world when over-crowded fishing boats drifted out to sea in search of freedom. The United Nations High Commissioner for Refugees created the Orderly Departure Program of 1979, with the objective of helping Vietnamese people leave their homeland safely and in an orderly manner. Applicants fell under one of three categories: 1) family unification abroad; 2) former US employee; or 3) former reeducation camp detainee. My father qualified under the third category. He was a Southern Republic soldier during the Vietnam War and held captive for five years. Two years after he applied, our family left Vietnam in 1993. My parents often talked about our lives before immigrating to the United States. I was not even three and had no memories of my life in Vietnam.

My earliest childhood recollections revolve around Edenvale Elementary School classrooms with holiday decorations and yuletide ornaments. I loved going to school around the holidays for the festive atmosphere because Christmas was quiet in our household of four, with no extended family in the United States. My teachers decorated the classroom with red and green everywhere and hosted endless Christmas art projects like making ornaments out of pine cones and uncooked macaroni. That extra effort from my teachers left a lasting impact. I cannot recall many adults from my childhood who were not relatives, but I remember my Edenvale teachers vividly. Even after leaving their classes, I liked to visit my elementary school teachers. My sixth-grade teacher, Carole Caputo, became someone I could talk to about worries that I could not communicate to my parents. I could not yet thoroughly express myself in English, and it was even harder to do so in Vietnamese.

Then in high school, my aerospace instructor lent his ears to my troublesome teenage years full of emotional confusion and anxiety. It became even more difficult to discuss these topics with my parents. The vast differences between where and how we grew up created a wall. We could not understand each other. Our values and opinions clashed. I was lucky to have my parents and other parental figures in my life to remind me of the importance of school and working hard, but there was still distance between us. For as long as I can remember, my decisions and endeavors were guided by a sense of awareness that my family was different from many other American families. My parents faced limitations that all immigrants had to confront. The most apparent was the language barrier.

We were lucky to live in San Jose, California, with a large and thriving Vietnamese community. There were Vietnamese supermarkets and grocery stores that sold familiar produce, but it was like a double-edged sword. My parents were not completely alone, but this comfort zone soon became a limitation because my parents grew afraid of the English language. They shied away from conversations with non-Vietnamese speakers. They feared for the lack of understanding between two cultures. My parents slowly reunited with friends and classmates from Vietnam, but there was an absence of the extended family support system that we longed for.

My parents had to work several jobs at the same time, often requiring manual labor. We were relieved when my dad finally found a job on the assembly line. In Vietnam, he was a law student prior to being drafted in the Vietnamese Army. After the war ended, my dad was detained into reeducation camps for five years. There were no options for veterans like him in Vietnam.

He came to the United States to build a new life for us. My dad did not know college was still an option for him. There were disadvantages stacked against immigrants, but we readily accepted them because we knew education was the golden ticket in America. That idea was my internal motivation to do well in school. I had drawn my own that my performance in school is the product of my parents' efforts. I could not let them down. My parents wanted to give me what they did not have or could not give me if we stayed in Vietnam. To them, a college degree was their American dream. It meant we were now equals to everyone else and no longer the inferior second-class citizens. A college education for me was a triumph over all the disadvantages that were stacked against my parents.

My parents believed a college degree would liberate me from the limitations they faced. Instead of choosing from limited options, I could create my own. This is not only my story to tell but one that belongs to millions of others. Growing up in immigrant families in the United States, my friends and I shared the same insecurities and challenges. As I stand in front of different students almost every day, I see the same stories in a few faces staring back at me.

Education levels the playing field for everyone regardless of background, gender, and ethnicity. Admission to college does not ensure success, and graduating from college does not guarantee employment. Nevertheless, college sets the foundation for boundless opportunities, especially when financial aid, work-study programs, and scholarships are available to families that would not otherwise be able to afford college for their children.

Traveling and living in Europe was something impossible that became a reality for me through college. The cost and logistics of visiting Europe were out of my parents' financial ability, but study-abroad programs made it possible. It was like a loophole that I never knew about. The whole process boiled down to filling out an application. In 2011, my summer vacation was drawn across seven warm weeks in Italy, followed by ten days of country hopping through Europe via train. Although my friends and I were stranded a few times in various train stations, the experience made for a good laugh. The end of summer came with three days of walking along the Seine River and reveling in the fact that my childhood dream came true.

The summer abroad helped me visualize America from my parents' perspective. I caught a sense of what my parents must have felt when they first arrived in the US—foreign language, homesickness; everything that was new and different was scary. I knew it was hard for them, but I did not comprehend how hard until I left home and experienced these feelings for myself. Before this trip, I struggled to understand why my parents were so cautious about everything. I finally came to the realization that they were overbearing and too protective because they were afraid. The language barrier and culture differences made any situation intimidating to them. This was especially the case when it was time for college applications. They wanted to help, but the entire process was as new to them as it was for me.

My understanding of college started with pen pal letters at Edenvale Elementary School. We would write to college students asking a myriad of questions, and they would write back to answer. Edenvale School hosted pancake breakfasts and spaghetti dinners to raise scholarship funds so that every sixth grader that graduated from high school could get a start in college. We had college students at school-wide assemblies speaking about their journey to college and the existence of financial aid, Cal Grants, scholarships, and work-study programs.

Personally, I do not believe students should have to feel pressure to prepare for college until in high school. However, from my own experience, the possibility of college should, nevertheless, be deeply rooted in those early elementary school years. When teachers consistently present higher education as something that is attainable, students are more likely to pursue their goals and dreams.

I owe it to my elementary school teachers to pay it forward for their efforts in helping me by helping future generations. That level of guidance and support is invaluable to immigrant families that are unaware of the resources available. My teachers provided an inclusive learning environment. They left their students with a sense of belonging. I hope to accomplish what they were able to achieve by believing in my students and laying the foundation for higher education.

As a teacher, my aspiration is to help kids connect with one another and others in the community. Students need to know that everyone is more alike than different. More importantly, I want my students to know there are people who believe in them and they are never alone in overcoming the obstacles they face. All it takes is one person who truly believes in them to change their lives forever.

At last, the end of the book. However, there is one more story that puts a frame around all the anecdotes you have read.

You Matter!

A beginning teacher was assigned to Edenvale Elementary School. The teacher was young and enthusiastic. I have seen a lot of teachers. Many of them became outstanding teachers. They had learned how to be excellent through training and experience. Only twice have I seen a "natural-born" teacher.

Hoa Nguyen was a natural! She did everything right. Every part of each lesson was full of good teaching practices that takes most of us a lifetime to learn. How to teach just came naturally to Hoa. Hoa made every lesson and every day special.

Each morning when the bell rings, students around the world line up in front of classrooms. As kids, we have all lined up thousands of times—nothing special, just routine. However, lining up in front of Hoa's classroom was not routine; it was special.

There were two rows of school bus yellow shoe prints painted on the asphalt in front of Hoa's room. When the bell rang, student hurried to class and stood on a pair of shoe prints. They stood quietly, just waiting for the day to begin. As soon as the students were lined up, Hoa would break into a huge smile. As each student walked by her, Hoa greeted each one by name, shook their hand, and made a positive comment specifically tailored to that child. What a way to start the school day!

I had never seen this practice, let alone from a first-year teacher. One day, I asked Hoa about it. Her answer was to the point.

"At the start of every school day, I make a personal connection with each child in my class. What I am really doing is saying, 'You matter!'"

What's the Point?

Treat every person with
dignity and respect,
no matter what!

TIKKUN OLAM

All it takes is one teacher to
completely change a youngster's life.
Why not be that teacher?